Fitzgerald, Hemingway, and the Twenties

Fitzgerald, Hemingway, and The Twenties

Ronald Berman

THE UNIVERSITY OF ALABAMA PRESS
Tuscaloosa and London

Manufactured in the United States of America

2 4 6 8 9 7 5 3 1
00 02 04 06 08 07 05 03 01

Typeface: Fairfield Light

∞

The paper on which this book is printed meets the minimum requirements of American National Standard for Information Science–Permanence of Paper for Printed Library Materials, ANSI Z39.48-1984.

Library of Congress Cataloging-in-Publication Data

Berman, Ronald.
Fitzgerald, Hemingway, and the Twenties / Ronald Berman.
p. cm.
Includes bibliographical references and index.
ISBN 0-8173-1057-6 (alk. paper)
1. Fitzgerald, F. Scott (Francis Scott), 1896–1940—Criticism and interpretation. 2. Hemingway, Ernest, 1899–1961—Criticism and interpretation. 3. American fiction—20th century—History and criticism. 4. Nineteen twenties. I. Title.
PS3511.I9 Z55774 2001
813′.5209—dc21
00-010158

British Library Cataloguing-in-Publication Data available

for Barbara

CONTENTS

Acknowledgments ix
Introduction 1

1 Cultural Drift: A Context for Fiction 11
2 "Bernice Bobs Her Hair" and the Rules 28
3 "The Diamond" and the Declining West 40
4 *The Great Gatsby* and the Good American Life 52
5 "The Killers" or the Way Things Really Are 65
6 Protestant, Catholic, Jew: *The Sun Also Rises* 82
7 Order and Will in *A Farewell to Arms* 99
8 Hemingway and Experience 116
9 Hemingway's Questions 132

Notes 149
Select Bibliography 167
Index 173

ACKNOWLEDGMENTS

Chapter 5 first appeared in *Twentieth Century Literature* 45, no. 1 (spring 1999). Chapter 6 first appeared in the *Hemingway Review* 18, no. 1 (fall 1998), copyright © 1998 by the Ernest Hemingway Foundation, all rights reserved.

Title excerpts from "The Swimmers," "The Diamond As Big As The Ritz, "The Ice Palace," and "Bernice Bobs Her Hair" by F. Scott Fitzgerald, reprinted by permission of Harold Ober Associates Incorporated (copyright as given by Charles Scribner's Sons in the original editions, not the 1989 collection).

Excerpts from "The Swimmers" reprinted by permission of Scribner, a Division of Simon & Schuster, from *The Short Stories of F. Scott Fitzgerald,* edited by Matthew J. Bruccoli (New York: Scribner, 1989), copyright © 1929 by the Curtis Publishing Company, renewed 1957 by Frances Scott Fitzgerald Lahahan. Excerpts from "The Diamond As Big As The Ritz," "The Ice Palace," and "Bernice Bobs Her Hair" also reprinted from *The Short Stories of F. Scott Fitzgerald,* edited by Bruccoli.

Excerpts from *The Sun Also Rises* by Ernest Hemingway, copyright © 1926 by Charles Scribner's Sons, renewed 1954 by Ernest Hemingway, and from *A Farewell to Arms* by Ernest Hemingway, copyright © 1929 by Charles Scribner's Sons, renewed 1957 by Ernest Hemingway, by permission of Scribner, a Division of Simon & Schuster.

Fitzgerald, Hemingway, and the Twenties

Introduction

This book is about the fiction of F. Scott Fitzgerald and Ernest Hemingway in the twenties. They came of age in this decade and did their best work in it. Scholarship has by now explained their lives, their sources, their professional interests, and the broad contours of their writing. We know about their place as men of letters in the twenties, and we have a reasonably good idea of their place in its history. But they were part also of its intellectual history, and that, I think, was problematic.

For some time now, we have realized that America in the twenties can not be fully described by social movements or political events. One is always surprised when reading accounts of the twenties to find how little they relate to *The Great Gatsby* or to *The Sun Also Rises*. Novels resist explanation in terms of their subjects. We cannot apply many valid generalizations—although more than those routinely invoked by the media. We tend to endow the decade of the twenties with a kind of unity it did not have: the "Jazz Age," once a splendid definition, has become a mass-market slogan.

The twenties were disintegrative. It was widely recognized that beliefs no longer rested on solid foundations, religious or secular, but novelists dealt necessarily with the nature of beliefs. God, church, doctrine, ritual and observance appear in the work of Fitzgerald and Hemingway, but in such a way as to let us know that something has happened to all of these entities. Here is one conclusion; it is from President Hoover's Research Committee on Social Trends in 1929: "If an American were to return to the United States after an absence of twenty years, he would note that, in our great cities at least, church buildings now appear trivial and unimportant in contrast with the enormous skyscrapers of commerce and finance. If he should happen to be of a speculative turn he might raise the question whether this development is a symbol."[1] Secular authority also experienced this loss of meaning and status. My aim in this book is to connect the work of Fitzgerald and Hemingway to the loss of certainty. What literary criticism has so far not done is examine the issues of philosophy, some of which were publicly debated, widely communicated.

Because this is a book of essays, no absolute connection exists between all subjects or texts that I cover. Nevertheless, the dominant themes of this inquiry are the way that fiction dealt with dogma both religious and secular; the new and old ideas of selfhood; and, especially in the case of Hemingway, the way we understand, explain, and transmit experience.

Before the Great War, the century had been peaceful but not placid; and the decade of the twenties was philosophically explosive. When Fitzgerald and Hemingway began writing, William James was still an intellectual force and H. L. Mencken was our leading critic. By the end of the twenties, James was an influential memory, Mencken had failed to adapt to modernism, and other voices like Edmund Wilson's were insistently being heard. Here is a recent view of the influence of James: "The problem . . . is where to draw the line, since his influence is felt in modern literature, sociology, political theory, psychology . . . philosophy. . . . James's thought comprised the crucial American contribution to the international matrix of early modernism. Along with Nietzsche, Bergson, Freud, Shaw, Ibsen, and Dostoevsky it was James whom the first self-conscious American cultural avant-garde—the young intellectuals of the generation of 1910—adopted as a hero in their revolt against Victorian and Puritan culture."[2]

Although less of a hero to the following generation, James had provided it with an intellectual horizon. What specifically had James achieved? As noted in the quotation above, his achievements might take several books to state. In my particular frame of reference, he made it allowable to think of life disconnected from any final authority—

although he was always conscious of and wistful for something that validated ideas and conduct. Both Hemingway and Fitzgerald were interested tactically in the operation of the conscious will in its field of action. They were, after all, also engaged in the pursuit of the American self in the American (and often the European) scene.

To write about those things was to enter a conversation already at a very high level. Josiah Royce observed that only Emerson and Jonathan Edwards could be compared to James, although internationally James had "a much more extended range of present influence than Emerson has ever possessed."[3] And Mencken wrote argumentatively that there was a great deal to learn about our culture from the philosophers: "George Santayana, despite his mysticism, described America vastly more realistically than Van Wyck Brooks."[4]

Describing America realistically means more than the photography of detail: for example, in "The Ice Palace" of Fitzgerald, Sally Carrol Happer says that she has "a sort of energy. . . . that may be useful somewhere."[5] Even in the backwater of Tarleton, Georgia, her terminology has its connections. That "energy" is, according to William James, the prerequisite for moral activity, for thought itself. To have it is to be in some measure heroic, and to lack it is to be—like most Americans. When Fitzgerald invokes the language of Jamesian will, he means for it to be noted. And when he repeatedly invokes languor and "drift" in *The Great Gatsby,* he introduces values antithetical to moral activity and will. From James through Walter Lippmann the term "drift" signified the refusal of Americans to live the conscious life of moral decision. Sally Carrol correctly perceives that the central issue of "living" is "*mind*" (emphasis added). Mind is action: she wants to leave the South because it is a place of "profound inertia." The South embodies James's problem of will; and its "spontaneous drift is towards repose."[6] The North too has its dangers, because it is a place where women are no less encouraged to lead lives of what James had called "nerveless sentimentality."[7] Fitzgerald's characters are drawn to emptiness.

"Bernice Bobs Her Hair" is an early story, and it too is concerned not only with the adventures of its characters but also with the ideas in their path. It is full of intellectual energies on display: one of its major figures has read many books that we too are expected to know or know about, and she is a priestess of social life. Marjorie is an exceptional analyst of American styles. She has the quantitative imagination that matters so much to Gatsby, to his author, and to American life in general, understanding all things in reference to the averages. Marjorie thinks the way that Santayana thinks that Americans think, in terms of appropriate numbers: she knows how many dances one should have and with how many men; how many ideas to cite and how near to go to the brink. She knows the difference between being interesting and being interested. Essentially, she is a formidable figure of the cultural marketplace.

When Bernice and Marjorie debate the values of *Little Women* and of the "modern girl" who can no longer live "like those inane females"[8] who so strikingly resemble their mothers, they participate in a larger dialogue. Mencken returned to the issue often during the late teens of the century and the early twenties. Marjorie has derived from him (he was a conduit for Ibsen and Shaw) the feminine quality of "sharp and accurate perception of realities . . . [and] a relentless capacity for distinguishing between the substance and the appearance." As Mencken noted a few years before Fitzgerald's story appeared, such a capacity was tactfully to be kept "from becoming too obvious" to men.[9] Mencken's admiring suspicion has as much to do with "Bernice Bobs Her Hair" as contemporary anxieties over The Younger Generation. But Marjorie's rationality, her marketplace mind, and her energies lead her to places neither she nor Mencken can navigate. Navigation is left to Bernice, who is in no respect more American than in the discovery of her subjective self. The story is, then, in more than one sense about outgrowing influences.[10]

"The Diamond As Big As The Ritz" continues Fitzgerald's use of Mencken, who was satirically interested in the lives and especially the style of the rich. But this story too goes considerably beyond him. Toward the end of *The Great Gatsby,* Nick Carraway says that he realizes it has been a story of the West, after all. The same might be said of "The Diamond," with certain complications. The West is also the west, or our civilization. It had come to stand for both meanings in the writings of Edmund Wilson and Van Wyck Brooks. In the years just before Fitzgerald wrote his short story, the played-out West was understood to represent American ideas and perhaps to anticipate American destiny.

The desolate village of Fish is our historical landscape seen in terms of entropy. A landscape in ruins signifies the collapse of nineteenth-century optimism. By the end of the story we are in a familiar place, another landscape in ruins that argues, metonymically, against current American confidence in destiny.

The idea of the good life in Braddock Washington's palace comes from a new philosophy. Everything in this place conforms to advertising image and copy: upscale ads of the early twenties consciously used gold, silver, jewels, tapestries, and enormously opulent cars to suggest that consumption might transform the middle class to an ideal form of itself. Washington's castle may be far away, but it remains the American scene, recognizably full of our material dreams. More important, it is dominated by a marketplace ethic that had recently been identified by Walter Lippmann: the translation of morals into new, crazily reasonable, businesslike forms. The reductive way that Braddock Washington thinks about things human is itself an issue of the twenties.

There are in *The Great Gatsby* a number of American Dreams. They derive from the Ur-dream of the New World as the state of renewed innocence; then from the dream of a chosen nation reaching its ordained form. Well into the twentieth century, it was assumed that individual dreams reflected these larger things, and the anachronistic Mr. Gatz still believes in the connection between his son's "big future" and national greatness. But a significant change had occurred in the idyll of democracy, and some of the least likely characters in the novel establish that. Myrtle Wilson, Meyer Wolfshiem, and Lucille McKee all participate in a dialogue of gentility. They suggest that some people are "below" others, that clothes do make the essential man, that a "gentleman" is at the top of the American scale. They and the Buchanans understand the operation of caste within plutocracy. The old democratic dream belonged to Jimmy Gatz; the new dream of monied style belongs to Jay Gatsby and to these voices of the early twenties. The new dream is centered on the change of identity through style, not works; hence the permeation of the novel by the commodity culture. Through the new dream, the old one is seen darkly. The excellence of things replaces human excellence, and it is a temptation not often resisted to do as Myrtle Wilson and Gatsby do, surround themselves with things. In

Myrtle's case, that allows her to purchase an identity with all its existential—and moral—components already in place, conferred so smoothly and easily by advertising.

Yet, when Gatsby tries to state his faith in the language of possessions, he is not simply admitting that he is a materialist—and so in his estimation is Daisy. He is saying that he knows no other language to express faith. This distinction had been articulated by Santayana in 1920 in an important *caveat* about the earth-bound dreams of Americans. As he saw it, there is a natural progression in this country from the spiritual to the material.[11] Gatsby may have immortal longings, but the only way he knows how to express them is through acquisition and display, through the American idea of success. Yet, although matter conceals spirit, spirit is still there.

The Sun Also Rises, which I address under the rubric of "Protestant, Catholic, Jew," debates the culture and nature of all three religions. I have raised a particular issue: it is usual to discuss Robert Cohn in terms of generic anti-Semitism, but some work remains to be done. He exists in this novel in relation to a certain kind of anti-Semitism—and to the ideologies of Catholicism and Protestantism.

Hemingway uses Catholicism as a benchmark of intellectual order in this novel. As Jake Barnes states, it provides the understanding of human character. But Catholicism was in the early twenties under a particular kind of attack and suffered from its own defense. The attack was mounted by H. G. Wells and other progressive minds who believed that the phrase "medieval" was pejorative. The Wellsian intent was to change and improve human organization and even human character. We know how resistant Jake Barnes is to that: it is one of the functions of his Catholicism. Ideas like those of Wells were disproved; however, the Catholic ideology of the twenties evolved by G. K. Chesterton and Hilaire Belloc produced its own problems. In order to assert their own values, they attacked both Protestants and Jews.[12] Belloc and Chesterton (along with Ezra Pound and T. S. Eliot) provided Hemingway with a strategic form of anti-Semitism. It was not the golf-club anti-Semitism practiced in, say, Oak Park at the turn of century. There was a full-blown theory that Jews are a foreign element in the culture of the West; that they cannot be absorbed; that their skepticism about values communicates itself everywhere; and, most important, that their own cultural style causes a principled, anti-Semitic reaction. That is why so much of *The Sun Also Rises* is about the guilt of the victim.

Nevertheless, *The Sun Also Rises* has an important twist: Robert Cohn is not despised entirely because he manifests Jewish values. He is, after all, romantic, chivalric, athletic; qualities that Jews may have, but not qualities they are accused of having. These are Cohn's masking qualities as Hemingway sees them: protective Protestant coloration for someone whose honor is compromised by an original Jewish character that cannot be changed. Real thought eludes Cohn, who is located somewhere on the intellectual scale between Horatio Alger and W. H. Hudson. He brings some brittle secular values to Pamplona with him: a vague belief in personal change, moralism about men and women, indifference toward the primitive authenticity of the bullfight—hence toward much else of historical value. He seems to have little of what in 1929 Reinhold Niebuhr called the sense of the tragic in human life, or any awareness of necessary failure.[13] The ideas that Niebuhr identifies are at the heart of *The Sun Also Rises,* and I think a great issue of the novel is its opposition to the new sentimentality exemplified by Robert Cohn. It might be called sentimental rationalism—and it is at work in more than one Hemingway piece.

The essence of "The Killers" is, I think, its extraordinary number and kind of questions. As in other stories like "Indian Camp" and "A Clean Well-Lighted Place," these questions set the interrogative *moral* mood. But a great effort has been made in "The Killers" to move the interrogation toward even larger issues. Far more than other stories, this one moves transparently from one kind of question to another. Its questions are first tactical but then metaphysical. "The Killers" is one of our great summations of invalidated ideas.

It is habitual for Hemingway to ask questions, but in "The Killers" we get advice from Max and Al that needs some reconstruction. We are by now so familiar or think we are so familiar with this story and its moment, that we forget what the attitudes were toward inquiry and how Hemingway addressed those attitudes. The asking of questions was, the

Public Philosophy said with great explicitness, itself a moral activity. One expected that they could be answered—and within the framework of a democratic understanding. Certain questions were important, such as those that addressed motive, universality, *and especially the meaning of action.* "The Killers" not only advises us to forget such questions; it also forecloses any answers. In this story we will get no answers about moral universals because they do not exist.

As Edmund Wilson had discerned shortly before "The Killers" was written, modern life seemed to be ever more characterized by logical pointlessness. Max and Al convey to Nick and George and Sam not only that life is complex and dangerous but also that their expectations about it are unreal. Like most Americans, they expect to see order and logic in the way things are; however, as William James had told his national audience, moral absolutes might be only assumptions.[14] Among the numerous points of pointlessness echoed by Max and Al, that one is most telling. It works, as Hemingway intended, to remove the basis for our social faith.

Much of what I have written concerns the relationship of writing to the thought surrounding it. In the case of *A Farewell to Arms,* there is an added complication. The novel deals with a number of intellectual time zones: the first decades of the century, which have provided the novel's characters with a basis for expectation; the disillusioning time of the Great War itself; and, equally important, the time in which the novel was written.

Edmund Wilson thought in 1928 that writing was entering a new national phase. Novelists were becoming solitary-minded and subjective, and in their stories "thoughts never pass into action."[15] It may be that Frederic Henry is not an intellectual casualty of the *war* but of the *twenties.* Hemingway has downloaded into the period of 1917–18 a good deal of insight accumulated in the period from 1918 to 1929. The political content of this novel would not have been possible without observation of Europe and America and particularly of Italy in the post-war decade. *A Farewell to Arms* contains many important political discussions, and they take their point from hindsight. Frederic Henry is able to dispute Socialist expectations, for example, because the experience of a decade, to say nothing about its coverage in the news, has given his author the right answers about political possibility. His surmises about post-war politics, especially Fascism, have already been validated. In certain respects, this novel deals with the romance of political belief the way that "The Killers" deals with moral sentimentality.

More than any other work I have looked at with the exception of *The Great Gatsby,* this novel relies on contemporary ideas. Frederic Henry keeps calling to our attention the ways in which his mind seeks unconsciousness and distance from experience. Wilson called this kind of current attitude the "discouragement of the will," and he connected it to the problems of modernism as the twenties ended.[16] Clearly, one of these problems was the difficulty of stating experience. One of the most difficult things to account for in Hemingway is the reluctance to discuss feeling and act.

It is important to place Hemingway within a tradition of inquiry that is skeptical and empirical. He made the dialogue of questioning central to his writing, and very little is exempt from it. *A Farewell to Arms,* a central intellectual document of the decade, takes up questions and the extrapolated idea of questioning in ways that go far beyond either war or romance. But this novel is not the only important work of the late twenties written in the interrogative mode. It arrives, after all, when Alfred North Whitehead, Bertrand Russell, and Ludwig Wittgenstein are debating contemporary explanations of human experience. Frederic Henry sees through systematic attempts to make experience intelligible, and this echoes philosophical debate. Looking backward, Russell recalled that 1917 was a highly meaningful year in which for him the disparity "of language to facts" first became clear.[17] He remarked dryly in 1927 that some of our most cherished ideas (including some ideas of William James) might be nothing more than "metaphysical superstition" or "delusion."[18] Whitehead gave a rubric to Hemingway and many others in arguing the dissolvent effect of science on religion, and Wittgenstein altered the very conception of the answerable.

These essays go back to the matrix of the decade of the twenties. I have relied on first-hand sources, which now need rediscovery. The ideas I have (selectively) outlined were dispersed in the first quarter of the century. Fiction connected to them, as it usually does, not through the structures of philosophical form but through intuitions and allusions carried by the winds of doctrine. Fitzgerald and Hemingway read many books, and they were alert to intellectual currents, especially to the contradictions of ideas and of ideologies. They were much concerned with the problem of untenable belief—and also with the need to believe.

1

Cultural Drift: A Context for Fiction

The Great Gatsby depends upon what William James had earlier called "the buzzing and jigging and vibration of small interests and excitements that form the tissue of our ordinary consciousness."[1] Fitzgerald's text alludes often to its surrounding world of things and ideas, demanding from the reader a sense of placement and allusion: he will particularize certain ideas about American national character. One of these ideas, developed over the first quarter of the century, concerns moral, emotional, and cognitive apathy. For example, *The Great Gatsby* systematically describes character and thought in terms ranging from indolence and inertia to withdrawal and paralysis. Daisy Fay Buchanan's languor is moral as well as stylistic; Jordan seems not only situationally "bored" but also existentially; background figures are sick or silent or "lethargic" or paralytically drunk—while the deadly heat of the book's last chapters refers itself to the dull unconsciousness of mind without will that had been stamped upon the historical moment by Eliot in 1922. There are witty reasons for so many of the characters of this novel and of *The Sun Also Rises* being exhausted, unthinking, or horizontal.

Nowhere is this kind of statement more referential than in Fitzgerald's use of the idea of personal—and national—"drift." The Public Philosophy of William James had formulated in that metaphor its sense of American failure. Tom and Daisy Buchanan are figures of fiction but also of American philosophy, a generation literally and figuratively at sea: "Why they came east I don't know. They had spent a year in France, for no particular reason, and then drifted here and there unrestfully wherever people played polo and were rich together. This was a permanent move, said Daisy over the telephone, but I didn't believe it—I had no sight into Daisy's heart but I felt that Tom would drift on forever seeking a little wistfully for the dramatic turbulence of some irrecoverable football game" (8–9).[2] To a contemporary reader, come of literary age as Fitzgerald did in the first quarter of the century, the conception was familiar. The Buchanans lead American lives of no moral or existential significance. They remind us of characters we have seen before in political and philosophical discourse who refuse to make choices or even to recognize the necessity for doing so. And yet, in the age of Theodore Roosevelt and William James, the active life opposed inert social complacency. The passage cited connotes unwilled compliance—its life rhythm is that of a tidal cycle, and we feel the organic rhythm of something less than human. The passage implies important unstated questions that will not be answered. Above all, there is the sense of psychological inertia. Lives may well be perceived in terms of an accidental course, with an accidental burden.

When Fitzgerald invokes languor, passivity, and the longing for unconsciousness, he refers himself to Eliot and also to the context upon which Eliot was dependent. There is a remark by Jacques Barzun on the fiction of Henry James, whose characters "work evil and cause harm . . . not because of what they desire but because of their heedless way of gaining it. . . . Even in his wonderful gallery of characters who are not evil but weak and shady, Henry shows that their need to deceive is a lack of power to feel the idea of decency."[3] Corresponding to this, formulated in a more systematic and I think more important way in the work of William James, are characters of philosophical dialogue. They are inert, as Barzun describes them, "adrift in experience."[4]

In the first quarter of the century James and other public philosophers had much to say about American issues. In his first series of *Prejudices* (1919) H. L. Mencken stated that James had in fact become the official conscience of the public, appearing "in every one of those *American Spectators* and *Saturday Reviews* at least once a week, and often a dozen times."[5] The sense of his moral leadership was, according to *Civilization in the United States,* "unanimous" because he "succeeded in deeply affecting the cultural life of a whole generation."[6] John Dewey, who succeeded James as national arbiter, was later described by Henry Steele Commager as "the guide, the mentor, and the conscience of the American people." Commager added that "it is scarcely an exaggeration to say that for a generation no issue was clarified until Dewey had spoken."[7] In addition to James and Dewey, others like Lippmann provided a context for fiction—and often invoked both poetry and novels.[8]

James himself wrote that "the spontaneous drift of thought" habitually defeated moral purpose. Men and women were naturally attracted to indifference, self-defensively imperceptive. But moral awareness had to be attained through concentrated consciousness, by an effort of focused attention that was "*the essential phenomenon of will.*" The function of human effort should be "to keep affirming and adopting a thought which, if left to itself, would slip away. It may be cold and flat when the spontaneous mental drift is towards excitement, or great and arduous when the spontaneous drift is towards repose."[9] The natural tendency to evade decision must continually be fought by the conscious play of mind. An entire creed is involved: first to concentrate upon the issue before us; then to deter the natural inconsistency of the mind; to adopt a reasonable conception of action and of self; and finally to translate decision into meaningful act. Above all was the display of "energy."

"Drift" denotes the moral unconsciousness of Americans at the turn of century. As James perceived the issue in the 1890s, the attractions of weakness were almost irresistible. He defined the idea of the heroic precisely by its opposition to intellectual and social inertia. Heroism was not simply high-mindedness or risk-taking (although both of these mattered) but the willingness to make choices and commit actions. It was rational and intellectual, dependent on a prior state of achieved consciousness: "the mind is at every stage a theatre of simultaneous possibilities. Consciousness consists in the comparison of these with each other, the selection of some, and the suppression of the rest."[10] Under mass democracy, however, it was altogether safer to go along with the herd, to claim the rights of individuality without ever validating them. A number of analogues in fiction will suggest themselves.

The idea of "drift" or the avoidance of consciousness and decision was used by Eliot, Fitzgerald, and Hemingway. In the background was continuous philosophical and psychological argument about our national character. Lippmann, for example, developed one particular idea about that national character in *Drift and Mastery* (1914). Like much of the Public Philosophy, this argument frames itself in small narratives, trying to account for the way that individual American characters are shaped. We read scripts for novels about failed American lives, about characters like those of Wharton subject to "power, position, pull, custom, weakness, oversupply, the class monopoly of higher education, inheritance, accident, the strategy of industrial war"; about lives out of Dreiser in "dingy little butcher-shops, little retail businesses with the family living in the back room, the odor of cooking to greet you as you enter the door, fly-specks on the goods—walk through any city."[11] From James through Lippmann to Dewey, there was insistence on the connection between philosophy, poetry, and fiction.

We ought, Lippmann writes, to choose design over accident, navigation over drift—but that becomes increasingly difficult in a mass democracy. The theme of current American life is passivity and even exhaustion: "Effort wells up, beats bravely against reality, and in weariness simmers down into routine or fantasy." Here is Lippmann on the contemporary American self: "This abandonment of effort is due, I imagine, to the fact that the conscious mastery of experience is, comparatively speaking, a new turn in human culture. The old absolutisms of caste and church and state made more modest demands than democracy does: life was settled and fantasy was organized into ritual and riveted by authority. But the modern world swings wide and loose, it has thrown men upon their own responsibility. And for that gigantic task they lack experience, they are fettered and bound and finally broken. . . . No wonder then that those who win freedom are often unable to use it; no wonder that liberty brings its despair."[12]

At some length Lippmann reconsidered James's ideas about the attractions of apathy. It might be noted that when James framed his issues, moral responsibility rested with individuals; but when Lippmann developed his own argument, it rested upon things, conditions, historical circumstances, which made his argument, to a certain extent, more useful to novelists and much more useful to political theory.

In *Drift and Mastery* Lippmann brought political theory up to date and provided for the literature of the twenties a useful set of encoded ideas. He observed first that we are "a nation of uncritical drifters." The context for American character is American history: "those who went before inherited a conservatism and overthrew it; we inherit freedom, and have to use it. The sanctity of property, the patriarchal family, hereditary caste, the dogma of sin, obedience to authority,—the rock of ages, in brief has been blasted for us. Those who are young to-day are born into a world in which the foundations of the older order survive only as habits or by default."[13] This statement might serve as a lucid commentary on the social thought of Fitzgerald and Hemingway. Its main themes infiltrate their work and appear in their lives.

Lippmann argues that Americans do not want to think for themselves or govern themselves. They fear independent lives and want only "to be taken in charge." It is a script in waiting for Daisy Fay Buchanan, who acts without passion because she "wanted her life shaped . . . by some force" (118). She may be a goddess, but she is also a representative American figure. Lippmann gives us the sense of an inevitable ending for that kind of figure: without an act of will, "all weakness comes to the surface" of American minds.[14] In short, he provided for the subsequent generation of writers a set of ideas about the looseness of American social organization, its severance from the old order, the pathetic incompetence of the new order as evinced in politics and social movements, and the reliance of American character upon its own limitations. It is a recipe for failure, and the fiction of the twenties is rich in the depiction of Americans unmade. The particular vein is the unwilling relationship of the individual to regnant social and ethical ideas.

Lippmann was widely available to writers through journals like the *New Republic*. A bridge to his ideas also existed in the work of Van Wyck Brooks, whose *America's Coming-of-Age* (1915) and *Letters and Leadership* (1918) criticized the arguments of James and Lippmann and brought them directly to the generation of Fitzgerald, Hemingway, and Edmund Wilson. In *Letters and Leadership* Brooks examined the idea of "drift," which he took to be "the general aimlessness of our life." He traced the analysis of this condition, correctly, to William James and Lippmann, describing the "pulp-like, inelastic state in which we find ourselves today." But Brooks was suspicious of pragmatism and of the

Public Philosophy. After all, William James was influenced by an essentially late-Victorian set of literary models, and although it was useful to read James, Lippmann, and Dewey on art, they were ultimately prosaic. According to Brooks, their analysis of our intellectual flaws was hopelessly behind the times. Culture is the responsibility of writers with more complex and inclusive tastes than William James or (to name another lover of late-Victorian poetry) Josiah Royce. Pragmatic intelligence was, Brooks wrote, simply not enough for literary understanding: it might lead eventually only to the mysticism of James, the civic religiosity of Dewey, and the bewilderment of everyone else.[15]

Using a familiar figurative language, Brooks described America when the twenties began as: "becalmed . . . on a rolling sea, flapping and fluttering, hesitating and veering about, oppressed with a faint nausea." The idea of "drift" extends itself into metaphor, prepares the ground for the meaningless voyaging and failed navigation of *The Waste Land* and *The Great Gatsby.* It also extends into metaphor the meanderings by automobile (Brooks sees Americans, themselves part of machinery-in-life, "driving about the country in Ford cars, on Sundays, . . . with their mouths open") that play so large a part in the symbolic realism of Sinclair Lewis.[16] When Babbitt and Kennicott set forth in their minutely described and passionately possessed cars, they often go nowhere. Lewis demands more symbolic reading than he usually gets.

In 1921 Fitzgerald tried to give some account of the suspicions of "the younger generation" about the Victorian past.[17] The phrase was much in use: Brooks had in 1918 combined it with the by-now intensely developed idea of cultural drift. He used a figurative language that conflicted with mainstream self-imaging. I think that he was quite aware that his choice of terminology contradicted—and rebuked—the understanding of American history to be found in *Harper's* or the *Saturday Evening Post.* Against a national *mythos* of frontier mastery, of imposing American *logos* upon nature, we suddenly find ourselves in a labyrinth as mysterious as Dante's. We are lost in historical time as well as in space:

> We of the younger generation . . . find ourselves in a grave predicament. . . . The acquisitive life has lost the sanction of ne-

> cessity which the age of pioneering gave it. A new age has begun, an age of intensive cultivation, and it is the creative life that the nation calls for now. But for that how ill-equipped we are! Our literature has prepared no pathways for us, our leaders are themselves lost. We are like explorers who, in the morning of their lives, have deserted the hearthstone of the human tradition and have set out for a distant treasure that has turned to dust in their hands; but, having on their way neglected to mark their track, they no longer know in which direction their home lies, nor how to reach it, and so they wander in the wilderness, consumed with a double consciousness of waste and impotence.
>
> I think this fairly describes the frame of mind of a vast number of Americans of the younger generation. . . . [who] drift almost inevitably into a state of internal anarchism.[18]

The passage frames its message in a sequence of historical and biblical metaphors. But one particular idiom matters a great deal, referring itself to nineteenth-century American history. In school texts, best-sellers, and newsstand publications, the pioneer experience had until recently been sacred. It was one of the great models for national life; we think of Babbitt, at one with Nature on his sleeping porch, comfortable in the assurance that civilization has not softened him. But this passage suggests that interior space is trackless. It is calculated to offend a nation of Pathfinders. It is also calculated to show what Brooks has been doing with the sources of his arguments: In 1911, Josiah Royce had asked, "What are the principles that can show us the course to follow in the often pathless wilderness of the new democracy? It frequently seems as if . . . we needed somebody to tell us both our dream and the interpretation."[19] One of the problems for modern readers is that they expect the American Dream of the first quarter of the century to be defined and accessible, but it is often described as unknowable.

The literature of the next decade, which featured so extensive a vocabulary of loss, drift, and unconsciousness, followed the example of Brooks, Lippmann, James, and others. There is a national context for lines like these from *The Great Gatsby:* "What'll we do with ourselves this afternoon . . . and the day after that, and the next thirty years?"

(92). At the same time that these lines appeared in print, John Dewey was lecturing on the "impotent drifting" that now pervaded American life and gave us a childish national character.[20] In *The Great Gatsby* we are not only intended to see the psychological state or moral metabolism of Daisy Fay Buchanan but also to be guided, by the language of description, to an idea about a new generation in America. Insistently, the novelists imply dimness of perception, unsteadiness of choice, absence of will, and a kind of "drift" of the imagination. We are intended to see at least part of the unity of writing in the first quarter of the century; the interdependence of language and idea among philosophers, poets, and novelists. To drift, in the literature just before and just after the Great War is to share unwillingly the experience of a generation that has nothing to rely on but itself. Drift means unanchored distance—to be at the mercy of currents like those that sweep so insistently through *The Waste Land.*

A pointed encounter between ideas occurs near the end of Edith Wharton's *The Age of Innocence.* In this novel so preeminently about the passivity of American will, the greatest of all adversaries to that state of mind appears within the text. Teddy Roosevelt's presence in *The Age of Innocence* (it is as if Eliot had introduced Sir James Frazer as a character into *The Waste Land*) may be realistic, but his inclusion is even more symbolic. The prophet of the active life suddenly shares the same page with the most hesitant, passive, and withdrawn figure in the fiction of the early twenties, Newland Archer:

> It was in that library that the Governor of New York, coming down from Albany one evening to dine and spend the night, had turned to his host, and said, banging his clenched fist on the table and gnashing his eye-glasses: "Hang the professional politician! You're the kind of man the country wants, Archer. If the stable's ever to be cleaned out, men like you have got to lend a hand in the cleaning."
>
> "Men like you—" how Archer had glowed at the phrase! How eagerly he had risen up at the call! It was an echo of Ned

> Winsett's old appeal to roll his sleeves up and get down into the muck; but spoken by a man who set the example of the gesture, and whose summons to follow him was irresistible.
>
> Archer, as he looked back, was not sure that men like himself *were* what his country needed. . . . [21]

We are intended, I think, to refer ourselves to another passage through which this one may be read, from Roosevelt's famous speech at the Sorbonne on the active life: "it is not the critic who counts; nor the man who points out how the strong man stumbles, or where the doer of deeds could have done better. The credit belongs to the man who is actually in the arena, whose face is marred by dust and sweat and blood; who strives valiantly. . . . who spends himself in a worthy cause." The peroration has a long literary history: "his place shall never be with those cold and timid souls who know neither victory nor defeat."[22]

The Age of Innocence, celebrated for its realistic mastery of the social life of the past, is also a novel of the twenties that, along with, say, *Main Street,* refers itself to issues of the kind I have described. Wharton's novel, like any other literary work, is both about the time in which it is set and the time in which it is written.[23] There are good and practical reasons for understanding it as a picture of Victorian America, but one might prepare for it by reading texts from *Pragmatism* to "Prufrock." Clearly, Newland Archer has been disarmed by gentility, and like certain characters of Henry James, he seems not to have the option of psychological change. He leads a conventional life because conventions matter so powerfully for him. But Archer, who appears as the twenties begin, has some of the characteristics of the cultural moment.

Archer has a great deal of trouble awakening and it might be suggested that Brooks's essay on "Our Awakeners" (1918) has some application. In this essay Brooks asks, "What, in fact, is the note of our society today?" His conclusion is that American life manifests "a universal tepidity," is morally a kind of vestige of Puritanism disarmed by sallow conscience, and "makes perhaps a majority of our kindly fellow-countrymen seem quite incapable of living, loving, thinking, dreaming or hoping with any degree of passion or intensity."[24]

There are two particular issues involved. Newland (if that is a place, he too is lost in it) Archer withdraws from the world of reforms and movements and fads and fetishes and frivolities but only into another kind of imitation of action. His own *vita activa* is designed to keep from living, loving, thinking, dreaming. The ending of *The Age of Innocence* is about the drift or inertia that characterizes American lives and also about self-imposed realities. Indeed the words "real" and "reality" direct us toward certain meanings in that ending. Archer withdraws (and withdraws once more into himself), protesting that it would be "more real" to stay away from Madame Olenska than it would be to enact his desires. He fears that "reality should lose its edge" if he undertook to qualify his sense of meaning by acting upon it. This will echo in Eliot's later line about humankind being unable to bear much reality. But the idea explored by Wharton and polished by Eliot began its modern journey in William James, who wrote that "the sense of reality," baffled by uncertainty, can only be asserted by a conscious act of "effort." Without that, we would drift from any supposed reality to any other. Brooks's essay of 1918 uses the same terminology: "observe the condition in which we now are: sultry, flaccid, hesitant, not knowing what we want and incapable of wanting anything very much, certainly not in love with our life, certainly not at home in this field of reality." It seems to be a script not for Victorian America, which had its certitudes, but for America on the verge of the twenties. Impulses and passions matter enormously: perhaps the main reason why Roosevelt is invoked by Wharton is that they have political, national counterparts. At any rate, Brooks clearly identifies the issues: the good American life is only possible if it proceeds from one's own "feelings and desires."[25] That is why Gatsby is so large a figure and Newland Archer so small.

By far the longest of Walter Lippmann's studies of *Public Persons* in America is that on Sinclair Lewis. Lewis was an ideal subject because the Public Philosophy was tuned to realism: there could be few modes superior for depicting and solving social issues. *Main Street* and *Babbitt* deploy themes familiar to the pragmatic critics of American "civilization." Belles lettres may be interested in other things, but the Public Philosophy was principally intent on the conflict between the active will of the individual and the inertia of the social mass. This is not to say that Lippmann was without a critical sense; he found a lot to dislike in Lewis.

The novels of Lewis follow lines of argument drawn in the previous decade. Lippmann, writing about Lewis in 1927, sounds very much like Van Wyck Brooks writing about American culture in 1918:

> The America of Mr. Lewis is dominated by the prosperous descendants of the Puritan pioneers. He has fixed them at a moment when they have lost the civilized traditions their ancestors brought from Europe, and are groping to find new ways of life. Carol is the daughter of a New Englander who went west taking with him an English culture. In Carol that culture is little more than a dim memory of a more fastidious society; it merely confuses her when she tries to live by it in Gopher Prairie. Babbitt is the descendant of a pioneer; he is completely stripped of all association with an ordered and civilized life. He has no manners, no coherent code of morals, no religion, no piety, no patriotism, no knowledge of truth and no love of beauty. He is almost completely decivilized, if by civilization you mean an understanding of what is good, better and best in the satisfaction of desire.[26]

In some respects, this is Brooks *redivivus,* with the original stating in 1918 that Americans have lost their pioneer inheritance but no longer possess "any other meaning." The younger generation in particular are without "a living culture, a complicated scheme of ideal objectives, upheld by society at large, enabling them to submerge their liberties in their loyalties and to unite in the task of building up a civilization."[27] A contemporary reader of Lewis would recognize some well-defined issues, among them the debate over civilization, the loss of authenticity of the pioneer tradition (to be expected in the age of Veblen and Beard), the failure of national American will locally exemplified, and everywhere in the texts a metaphorical sense of blindness, unconsciousness, "groping," dimness, and drift.

At exactly the same time, 1920, two women appear in American fiction, both condemned by their authors to live in Minnesota: Carol Kennicott of *Main Street* and Sally Carrol Happer of "The Ice Palace." Their lives have a plot, that of the active individual will against the inert social mass. Carol Kennicott is a version of the Progressive political will who "wanted, just now, to have a cell in a settlement-house, like a nun without the bother of a black robe, and be kind, and read Bernard Shaw, and enormously improve a horde of grateful poor."[28] If one model is Shaw, the other is Jane Addams of whom Lippmann made an important distinction: "She was not only good but great." According to Lippmann, she exemplified democracy at its best and should be compared not to figures of charity but to those of American politics; in fact, he adduces Lincoln.[29] Jane Addams had a considerable importance for American Public Philosophy as a symbol of the *vita activa,* and she figures in the ideas of John Dewey.[30]

Some of the changes proposed by Carol Kennicott are merely cultural and hence enjoy a kind of amiable, female unimportance. But some have to do with social and public issues, which register bigger waves on the American seismograph. It is bad enough to be, like the other women in town, "twice as progressive as the men"; but it is worse to argue about school bonds or a farmers' co-operative; and it is impossible to state actually political opinions about land use or any issue not on the Republican ticket.[31] The active will becomes deflected into the lesser business of mind and art, into the deliberations of the Thanatopsis Club and the infantilism of "The Girl from Kankakee"—a play chosen to exorcise the influence of GBS over Carol's overheated mind.[32]

Carol Kennicott and Sally Carrol Happer are prototypical figures of "the younger generation" at war with American society and mind. The latter reminds us (William James in Tarleton, Georgia) that she has "a sort of energy. . . . that may be useful somewhere" (51).[33] Nevertheless, the two women may become, if they do not will otherwise, figures of drift, silence, and withdrawal. For Lewis, the idiom in use for the past two decades is still current. For example, Guy Pollock, a relic of Gopher Prairie, with sympathy drawn from his own experience, tells Carol about the advisability of retreating from action into much safer "dullness and contentment." He has himself learned silence and divested himself of personality, which reduces social conflict and allows him to make quite a good living without actually competing for it. Perhaps the best thing that Carol can do is imitate him, learn to be "satisfied to be—nothing." The penalty for this kind of life, however, is occasional if private clarity: Pollock understands that his life is in effect "the biography of a living dead man." It is an important dialogue: As James had noted, the advice that Pollock gives about loss of self has its comfort, even its profit. At a later point Carol does experience this prudential, willed unconsciousness:

> She felt old and detached through high-school commencement week, which is the fete of youth in Gopher Prairie; through baccalaureate sermon, senior parade, junior entertainment, commencement address by an Iowa clergyman who asserted that he believed in the virtue of virtuousness. . . . Her head ached in an aimless way.
>
> In the prairie heat she trudged along unchanging ways, talked about nothing to tepid people, and reflected that she might never escape from them.
>
> She was startled to find that she was using the word "escape."
>
> Then, for three years which passed like one curt paragraph, she ceased to find anything interesting save the Bjornstams and her baby.

For those "three years of exile from herself," Carol, like Newland Archer, gives up on the issue of reality.[34]

Fitzgerald's Sally Carrol resists that fate, refuses "to be frozen, heart, body, and soul." The South may be "enervating," but the particular hell of the upper middle class ("she felt things creeping, damp souls that haunted this palace, this town, this North" [68]) is where the active life—another form of tedium diagnosed by William James—masquerades as real life. For both Fitzgerald and Lewis, the frozen North is a metaphor that extends the boundaries of realism.

Fitzgerald used and adapted the idiom of the cultural moment, but he was more complex than Lewis and more complex than Mencken really wanted novelists to be. Perhaps one reason why Mencken approved of Sinclair Lewis but had reservations about Fitzgerald, is that Lewis got his marching orders right, producing straightforward satire; Fitzgerald persisted in ambiguities. He was ready to think about the

South as if it did have some form of moral "energy" to go along with its civilized failures. That idea is denied furiously by Harry Bellamy, who is full of prejudices from *Prejudices* about Southern culture and its clear inferiority to the North: "They're sort of—sort of degenerates—not at all like the old Southerners. They've lived so long down there with all the colored people that they've gotten lazy and shiftless. . . . of all the hangdog, ill-dressed, slovenly lot I ever saw, a bunch of small-town Southerners are the worst!" (62–63).

The idea of a civilization wrecked by history takes a newly specific shape. The ideas have been absorbed by Fitzgerald—and by Harry Bellamy. Mencken's "The Sahara of the Bozart" had appeared in 1917 to much debate and was reprinted in *Prejudices: Second Series,* 1920. In this famous essay Mencken had described the South in contemptuous terms of mental "lethargy" and "torpor."[35] He had argued that the old Southerners have been displaced and that the "aristocracy" (a class much on Harry's mind) has disappeared.[36] Also in 1917, in another essay Mencken wrote of southern decline, fall, and social entropy: "The politics of the region is vapid and idiotic. . . . Its philosophy is the half supernaturalism of the camp-meeting. . . . Add to this intellectual emptiness, a bellicose and amusing vanity, and you have a picture of incompetence that is almost tragic. The whole machinery of so-called southern chivalry, the invention of the feudal aristocracy of ante-bellum days, now almost wholly extinct, has been taken over by the emancipated poor white trash."[37]

Harry Bellamy's argument is derivative: like Mencken, he worries greatly about the demise of the Southern "aristocrat" and argues that the "energy" for moral decision has disappeared below the Mason-Dixon line. So far, so good: he has objectively distanced himself and the North from the South. But Mencken's phrases have more than one application: "intellectual emptiness" and "bellicose and amusing vanity" are native to Harry Bellamy and to the frozen North. That is the tendency of much of the dialogue. Bellamy seems not only to outdo the boosters of Gopher Prairie but to anticipate those of Zenith. The latter, far more ideological, understand precisely what it is they defend. The issue in *Babbitt* as in Fitzgerald's story is by no means compliant inertia; it is active collusion in a civic ideology. The story warns us not only about the melancholy

North but also about a girl from the South who once failed uncritically to love it.

The tirade that seems to well up from Harry Bellamy's subconscious means a good deal: he has been engaged with his own long-standing problem, that of belonging to an aristocracy of money. The past is for him unsafe terrain because he knows what he will find there, a blank after three generations. He himself has no historical existence—which may be why he has such a strong reaction to the idea of a real American aristocracy, however diminished. The volcanic way in which the argument begins indicates that it has *been* an argument long before its statement, needing only an occasion.

The ending describes Sally Carrol's own "furious, despairing energy" (67) as she tries to break through the imprisoning ice. The language is both literal and figurative: "She was alone with this presence that came out of the North, the dreary loneliness that rose from ice-bound whalers in the Arctic seas, from smokeless, trackless wastes where were strewn the whitened bones of adventure. It was an icy breath of death; it was rolling down low across the land to clutch at her" (67). John Kuehl has stated that "images of heat and cold" are related to those of "inertia and energy."[38] The effects are various, and the cumulative effect of frigidity in all of its shades of meaning challenges notation:

> cold. . . . wraith of loose snow . . . mist. . . . chilling away the comfort. . . . sleet. . . . snow on her grave. . . . great piles of it all winter long. . . . crust . . . drifts . . . melting. . . . flakes. . . . cold. . . . a transparency of white. . . . ice. . . . icicled windows. . . . Ice was a ghost . . . pale faces and blurred snow-filled hair. . . . ice cave. . . . crystal walls. . . . caves of ice. . . . glittering. . . . opalescent, translucent. . . . icy sides. . . . white breath. . . . gray pagan God of Snow. . . . shimmer. . . . ice-bound . . . whitened bones. . . . icy breath of death. . . . freeze to death . . . embedded in the ice like corpses . . . preserved until the melting of a glacier. . . . all tears freeze up here. (64–68)

More than the death of the body is implied. These images combine the materials of poetry drawn from sources as distant as Coleridge's "Kubla

Khan" (and, I think, also his "Ancient Mariner") with the materials of the philosophy of vital energy.

By the time this story appeared, the intellectual world knew that energy referred to consciousness and will—two important qualities embodied in the heroine of this story. The matter is not simply existential: The good life was inherently the life of action based upon reflection; that was what made it social. One of the most disappointing things about our discovery of the North, along with Sally Carrol, is that it does not value the individual will; therefore, it has no authentic social existence. The body is frozen and so is the body politic.

Roger Patton, who like Guy Pollock in *Main Street* is a voice of reflective experience, has already said, "I used to have a theory about these people. I think they're freezing up" (59). Implicit in his metaphorical advice is the (silent) recognition of long winters of the soul among acquisitive Americans as well as among long-suffering Scandinavians. The story cuts two ways because the North too is a figure for unconsciousness. To use the phrase of Van Wyck Brooks, "the acquisitive life"—which I take to be the life of the North, Harry Bellamy's life, the social life expressed throughout the story so powerfully in terms of things and success and status—is just as much a form of unconsciousness as the Lotus-eating of the South. It can be safely described under the rubric applied by Mencken to the South, intellectual emptiness defended necessarily by bellicose vanity. In escaping the North for the South, Sally Carrol challenges the temptation of being neutralized by custom, or as Fitzgerald implies about the other women in this American place, made "devoid of personality" (61). The text, after all, has already warned us (have we ever read Ibsen?) that the Ice Palace may be A Doll's House.[39]

I have suggested that an idea of cultural landscape was on the mind of critics and writers. There is more to say about this, and my chapter on "The Diamond As Big As the Ritz" will suggest that Fitzgerald developed the idea. "The Ice Palace" is both literally and figuratively about losing one's way in America, groping for direction, enduring the subtle forms of moral and existential unconsciousness. It is also about finding the way back: "following a wide passage. . . . like the green lane between the parted waters of the Red Sea" (67). That word "green" should alert us to language and idea reincarnated in 1925 in *The Great Gatsby.* That too is associated with a kind of vitality of mind and will.

Fiction usually describes experience through metaphor, but in this story, metaphor is actualized as experience. It had taken a number of years for ideas of passive drift, inner coldness, and loss of self to become attached to life in America. When they became available, Fitzgerald knew what to do with them. What remained a metaphor for social thought became for him the structure of an experience, and he wove the opposition between inertia and consciousness into narrative.

2

"Bernice Bobs Her Hair" and the Rules

In 1920, George Santayana stated that "to be an American is of itself almost a moral condition, an education, and a career." If that is the case, then every stage will be a rite of intellectual passage. And, Santayana warned, in America "the milk of human kindness is less apt to turn sour if the vessel that holds it stands steady, cool, and separate, and is not too often uncorked."[1] We rise or change or affect our various conditions, but necessarily against those intent upon keeping us in our places. "Bernice Bobs Her Hair" is clear on that point because "the right to walk unchallenged" in the starry heaven of popular girls is only half-metaphorical. Mencken, also in 1920, put the matter this way: one has to enter American society "insidiously," before the portcullis comes crashing down.[2]

Entrance into Fitzgerald's story is entrance also into the upper middle class. There is constant allusion to the cost of arrangements rather than the cost of commodities. And there is constant scrutiny by the guardians of those arrangements, it being difficult to cross the country-club barrier of those "sharp eyes and icy hearts" (Santayana had it philosophically and metaphorically right) that detect authentically *haute bourgeois* character. This scrutiny will be repeated when Bernice is judged for her own deviations. In a middle class with sharply defined levels—and in a democracy with a heavy touch of oligarchy—all acts are witnessed.[3] The subtle differences in class and especially in status are largely the story's subject.

In "Bernice Bobs Her Hair" the location is a middling town and its "shifting semicruel world of adolescence" (26). Louis Raymond Reid's essay on "The Small Town" in *Civilization in the United States* (1922) was soon to argue that "small-town realism with a vengeance" had been the key to the success of "the young novelists . . . during the past year." As he puts the issue, "Riverside Drive, Fifth Avenue, Beacon Street, Michigan Boulevard, and Pennsylvania Avenue. . . . are not spiritually different from Main Street." So, fiction ought to deal with towns and cities in identical ways. Reid's view, self-consciously modern, dismissed the older (and to many Americans more persuasive) view that provincial life was different from and notably better than urban life. For example, Morton White has described prewar social philosophy in terms of its attachment to the town and its opposition to the unknowable modern city. White cites Josiah Royce among those who believed that "the problematic life of the nation as a whole" might be improved by renewing our original provincial values.[4] The squalor, corruption, and materialism of the metropolis were not to be encountered in the life of American towns. Fitzgerald is of two minds on this issue: There are times when the provinces are uncritically situated in his work; but when he needs conflict, even in Tarleton, Georgia, a country location exempts very little. In this case Fitzgerald finds the new decade to be as intensely present in the provinces as anywhere else. Bernice and Marjorie are connected to those Athenian centers of American civilization—New Haven, Williamstown, and Princeton—that are way stations to Chicago and New York. Roberta Dillon is as well known as Ty Cobb in the civilization of those who matter.

There is a story or a fragment of one for each character introduced in "Bernice Bobs Her Hair," but because "every one was Who's Who to every one else's past" (26), the stories have the same taxonomy. Bessie MacRae has been the life of the party, but for a little too long; Jim Strain and Ethel Demorest, mooning around for years without a red penny, have to trade time for money: "[They] had been privately engaged for three years. Every one knew that as soon as Jim managed to hold a job for more than two months she would marry him. Yet how bored they both looked, and how wearily Ethel regarded Jim sometimes, as if she wondered why she had trained the vines of her affection on such a wind-shaken poplar (26)."

The small events of Bernice's life are set against larger issues of making money and maintaining status. But always there are witnesses to strength and weakness and a sense that private life is played out in public. Fitzgerald's great "provincial" theme is not the current marketplace theme that life in small towns is deeply repressed, or that it is materialistic in the way that urban life is; his small towns are mirrors of class and caste in democracy.

One of the great comic lines in Fitzgerald is only three words long: Marjorie enters, "radiant as usual" (27). It is a crux, because as any dictionary will note, that is only possible for a source of light. The rest of us have to make do with occasional emissions of emotional energy, unless we are (as Marjorie is) monumentally theatrically accomplished. Of itself, nothing Newtonian can be radiant as usual. A reason for the illusion exists: Marjorie, although the most intelligent and accomplished of women, has little freedom of action, and she must work through others like Warren McIntyre and Otis Ormonde. We read from the beginning the difficulty of an intelligent woman accomplishing anything. Intelligence is not a provincial virtue, but it may be disguised by radiance—in its social form a response to the majority. Behind much of the action is the idea of "being popular," which depends not on the possession of an inherent quality but on a decision by a majority. Popularity is Fitzgerald's equivalent to politics.

Marjorie has a good, cold mind. For a while she will be the hero of the story: she "never giggled, was never frightened, seldom embarrassed, and in fact had very few of the qualities which Bernice considered appropriately and blessedly feminine" (29). She dislikes women and enjoys men. Above all, she is rational and will go as far as unaided reason can go, although Fitzgerald will point out its limits. That constitutes a second great subject of the story.

Quantities jostle each other, "position" works against "pulchritude," and "attention" is bought by entertainment. Marjorie lectures unceasingly about tactical ends, but their field of action is small. To work out the problems of sex, the preliminary matters of status, wealth, and approval must be negotiated. Freedom of action is something of an illusion.

Fitzgerald will quantify social facts: We know from the opening line of "Winter Dreams" that "poor as sin" means a one-room house, and that Dexter Green's status is completely defined within a clause: His father owned "the second best grocery-store in Black Bear."[5] Bessie MacRae has been the life of the party for more than ten years; Jim and Ethel have been engaged for three years hoping that he can hold a job for more than two months; Bernice wonders for the hundredth time why she is happy only in Eau Claire. The text responds with some precision: her family, "the wealthiest" in town, has calculated all "the factors in . . . social success" (29–30). Marjorie wants to look like a million while Bernice thinks about not having a red penny. Bernice knows that something is due to her condition in life and also that any condition can be cheapened. Like much else in this story, popularity has a market price.

The upper middle class counts everything, and its equation tends to be envy: Sarah Hopkins would "give ten years of her life and her European education to be as popular as Marjorie" (31), which is to say that it might well be a fair trade. Marjorie likes having three or four men cutting in every few feet, but real money might have gotten her to Paris instead of New Haven.

All things are located numerically within what Fitzgerald perceives to be America's universal language: a girl should be cut in on frequently; boys prefer to dance a dozen times an evening with butterflies, although one full fox-trot with the same girl is distasteful; a month's allowance for Marjorie will pay for a week at any hotel for Bernice; the best disguise for intelligence is to look like a million dollars; three sad birds that dance with you on one night add up, Platonically, to the right amount. We note finally, in this quantified social world, that Bernice will bob her hair in the first chair at the Sevier Hotel barbershop. That is the way the text is shaped because that is the way the middle class thinks. Fitzgerald had perfect pitch on this issue.

Mrs. Harvey has a notable opinion about a closed market: "When she was a girl all young ladies who belonged to nice families had glorious times" (30). The external narration is wickedly faithful to the unreflecting blankness of her mind. We see the social world—a very small place—from inside that mind. It is a sentence from which all objectivity has been leached out. Those phrases "nice families" and "glorious times" have had their Victorian life span, which Fitzgerald has just ended. They cannot be taken any more seriously now than the solipsistic Mrs. Harvey.

Status needs self-identifying knowledge as well as style, and ideas about men and women are often asserted. This is after all a story about education. Later in the decade, Fitzgerald was to write about the way we learned things. Speaking of Josephine in "First Blood" he restated "Dr. Jung's theory that innumerable male voices argue in the subconscious of a woman, and even speak through her lips."[6] In "Bernice Bobs Her Hair" the conception of the subconscious is also important, even dominant. Certain passages cross totemic boundaries. In the first of these Bernice acts the way she has been taught by books:

> "Do you want me to go home?"
>
> "Well," said Marjorie, considering, "I suppose if you're not having a good time you'd better go. No use being miserable."
>
> "Don't you think common kindness——"
>
> "Oh, please don't quote 'Little Women'!" cried Marjorie impatiently. "That's out of style."
>
> "You think so?"
>
> "Heavens, yes! What modern girl could live like those inane females?"
>
> "They were the models for our mothers."
>
> "Yes, they were—not! Besides, our mothers were all very well in their way, but they know very little about their daughters' problems." (33)

The conversation about books takes place in a library as symbolically located as the library in *The Great Gatsby;* if Bernice had her way the conversation would follow a script taken from novels. She would emote, Marjorie would follow certain "cues" self-evident in female literature, and sweet, sentimental reasonableness would ensue. Everything has a script. None of this happens; we find instead that Marjorie has other texts on her mind.

Louisa May Alcott serves the same purpose in this story as Horatio

Alger does in *The Great Gatsby.*[7] Fitzgerald has not always amiable contempt for the "models" of womens' literature and also for those who believed in them. Relics of Victorianism are often described by Fitzgerald as mindless, negligible, or senile. This is not entirely personal: the strategy was perfected by Jane Austen in order for the reader to perceive history through biography. Throughout Fitzgerald's work in the twenties, late Victorians remain visibly and necessarily present, their style and ideas summarized in a Mrs. Harvey or Mr. Gatz.

Marjorie's lecture on modern times continues, against the American grain:

> The lids of Bernice's eyes reddened.
>
> "I think you're hard and selfish, and you haven't a feminine quality in you."
>
> "Oh, my Lord!" cried Marjorie in desperation. "You little nut! Girls like you are responsible for all the tiresome colorless marriages; all those ghastly inefficiencies that pass as feminine qualities. What a blow it must be when a man with imagination marries the beautiful bundle of clothes that he's been building ideals round, and finds that she's just a weak, whining, cowardly mass of affectations!"
>
> Bernice's mouth had slipped half open. (34)

Bernice is not the only slack-jawed witness: the effect is exactly that hoped for by H. L. Mencken, one of those men on and perhaps in Marjorie's mind. In the February 1920 *Smart Set,* Mencken jeered at the mere "primping and decorating" of American women. Later, Marjorie may well have been on *his* mind: in the October 1921 issue he restates her theory of affectations: "A husband, after all, spends relatively few hours of his life parading his wife, or even contemplating her beauty. What engages him far more often is the unromantic business of living with her—of listening to her conversation . . . of facing with her all the dull hazards and boredoms of everyday life. In the discharge of this business personal beauty is certainly not necessarily a help; on the contrary, it may be a downright hindrance, if only because it makes for the hollowest and least intelligent of all forms of vanity. Of infinitely more value is a quality that women too often neglect, to wit, the quality of simple amiability."[8]

Mencken's contribution to Fitzgerald's conception of Marjorie (and to her dialogue) includes, I think, the following: a 1918 essay arguing that it was the masculine fate to be manipulated by superior female intelligence; a second 1918 essay on "the feminine talent for persuasion and intimidation"; a 1918 newspaper column that explicitly contrasted the current problems of women with those of their grandmothers; and a 1919 essay on the "deadly matter-of-factness" of American schoolgirls and their mastery of all the new and bewildering forms of "information."[9] Perhaps the most consistent of Mencken's arguments, running through these and many other pieces, is that the female mind is completely logical and equally completely unsentimental. It looks at things as they actually are and misses no detail. It certainly misses no detail about the working of the mind, as Marjorie demonstrates:

> "Do you mean to say that men notice eyebrows?"
> "Yes—subconsciously." (35)

Marjorie, who is superrational, has an easy, analytical contempt for something much larger, more dangerous, than she imagines. Part of the experimental nature of the story is its depiction of those processes that are beyond her imagination.

As to reasoning, there is a brief but important passage of Mencken's that in 1924 states that women are far too realistic to have any respect for ideas. They are happy to put up with any "idiotic theorizings on any subject" that men can contemplate, "whether theological, economic, epistemological or political."[10] That seems to have been anticipated by Marjorie's approach to those entirely equivalent subjects, Lenin, Wilson, and ping-pong:

> "I hate dainty minds," answered Marjorie. "But a girl has to be dainty in person. If she looks like a million dollars she can talk about Russia, ping-pong, or the League of Nations and get away with it."

"What else?"
"Oh, I'm just beginning! (35)

Marjorie, like Mencken, states that any idea in the masculine realm can be engaged. By doing so, she makes it clear that all such ideas have the same gravity. The triplet of "Russia, ping-pong, or the League of Nations" ensures that we get the point: none of these things matters any more than any other. Things in the realm of male opinion are as unserious as this sequence or as those pondering them. Without wasting much anxiety Marjorie appropriates the language of masculinity: if you can follow a clumsy man across a dance floor, then "you can follow a baby tank across a barb-wire sky-scraper" (35). And, if necessary, you can even rely on a soon-to-be famous novel of 1920: Marjorie has been reading Oscar Wilde because Amory Blaine has been doing the same thing, enjoying the intellectual prestige of skepticism.[11]

But there is more appropriation of language going on than we may realize. Bernice has been thinking over her initial social success, and she realizes that it was not entirely the work of the puppet-master: "But a few minutes before she fell asleep a rebellious thought was churning drowsily in her brain—after all, it was she who had done it. Marjorie, to be sure, had given her her conversation, but then Marjorie got much of her conversation out of things she read. Bernice had bought the red dress, though she had never valued it highly before Marjorie dug it out of her trunk—and her own voice had said the words, her own lips had smiled, her own feet had danced. Marjorie nice girl—vain, though—nice evening—nice boys—like Warren—Warren—Warren—what's-his-name—Warren—— She fell asleep" (39).

The subconscious plays an important role in a sequence of maneuverings against rational intent. There is more than tactical meaning in its invocation. First, if Bernice is to be inaugurated into a new self at a new time she has to experience new thought. Psychology was in the midst of the transition from James to Freud, from the consideration of the moral to instinctual domination. It took on new, even preeminent intellectual status. This was plainly recognized by Josiah Royce, who wrote that "the new psychology" is about more than mind. It is "a movement closely connected with all that is most vital in recent civilization, with all the modern forms of nationalism, of internationalism, of socialism, and of individualism. Human life has been complicated by . . . new personal and social problems."[12] Second, psychology is both a subject in this story and a way of understanding its happenings. Nothing could be more indicative of the idea of change *than the kind of change this story undergoes.* It begins by assuring the readers that they are on familiar ground, that class and money are self-evident indicators of identity, and that blunt realism explains all. But, half-way through the narration Bernice *really* begins to dream, that is to say, she sees things the way that the new psychology sees them. The argument takes place among books, but other revelations take place in bed.

From the beginning, the language has promised transactional possibilities. We can go to the dance if we are sufficiently middle-class; we can be popular in Eau Claire if matters are prudentially arranged; we can get married by holding down a job; we can be popular if we read the right texts and have the right conversations. Yet, the story is necessarily a critique of Marjorie's pure reason. The passage cited describes thought and feeling that are not only subrational but "rebellious," a term lifted out of Freud. The dream of Bernice shows the authenticity of the unconscious, whereas the artifice of Marjorie's "conversation" pointedly does not derive from the inner self. That "conversation" is set against Bernice's "own voice." The passage suggests that the sleep-world describes truths to us that are not always consciously visible. It argues the primacy of the Ego. It warns us against finding reality in texts; here reality is the work of unconscious verification. Marjorie, the preacher against vanity, is herself vain. The sequence of thought and feeling moves quickly from Marjorie to Warren, where it belongs. Freud cites with approval his predecessor Hildebrandt: Dreams at "their most sublime as well as their most ridiculous . . . borrow their basic material either from what has passed before our eyes in the world of the senses or from what has already found a place somewhere in the course of our waking thoughts."[13]

There is the symbolism of finding a red dress within a Freudian trunk. (*The Interpretation of Dreams* was reprinted seven times between 1900 and 1920.)[14] Fitzgerald's story had its first run in the *Saturday Evening Post* but might have served as a case history in psychiatry. It is about two women severing ties with their mothers and competing sexually while hiding their motives from each other and themselves. Marjorie already knows that although "our mothers were all very well in their way" they are necessarily displaced by time—and by their daughters. Bernice discovers her own motivation while asleep, taking Warren McIntyre's imago into her bed. Both girls are forcibly inducted into another stage of life. Susan Beegel reminds us of how this story modernizes the hidden sexual themes of *Little Women,* in which long hair is a sign of restraint: "When Bernice bobs her hair, a 'little woman' dies in the barber's chair and a flapper is born. . . . she severs herself symbolically from the Victorian ideal of womanliness." Something "snaps" in Bernice after her haircut—the last ties, one imagines, to "her Victorian upbringing."[15]

At least as interesting as totem and taboo is the great Freudian issue of embarrassment. At times the *real* activity of this story seems to be a dream, full of anxiety and rejection. As for being unveiled in all one's nakedness, there is that great moment with Draycott Deyo, who is studying for the ministry. Bernice tells him that "It takes a frightful lot of energy to fix my hair in the summer—there's so much of it—so I always fix it first and powder my face and put on my hat; then I get into the bathtub, and dress afterward. Don't you think that's the best plan?" Deyo might be better positioned to debate the possibility of life on Mars. His sputtering response can barely be followed because Fitzgerald's prose so closely imitates the unlubricated movement of his mind: "Though Draycott Deyo was in the throes of difficulties concerning baptism by immersion and might possibly have seen a connection, it must be admitted that he did not. He considered feminine bathing an immoral subject, and gave her some of his ideas on the depravity of modern society" (39). It is an explosion in a syllable factory. As Deyo lurches into thought, Fitzgerald invokes for him all those pontificating nouns that allow us to disguise images. If what we have just read is Deyo's own psychic language, then he really has done the work of the superego, translating Bernice's body into a cloud of harmless words. There may well be "the familiar though unrecognized strain of Marjorie in Bernice's conversation" (40), but this part of her dialogue corresponds more to intuition. By now, Bernice knows who is liable to dream what.

The moment long foreseen arrives and Bernice *literally* is challenged to make good her claim to sexual and social equity. First, the sexual conflict: Bernice denies that she wants Warren—but feels "suddenly and horribly guilty" (41) over his possession. As in a dream Bernice is silent, virtually paralyzed before Marjorie's unearthly powers of reason and articulation; she is, in fact, "completely incapacitated" (41). And as in a dream she has nothing to say against a chorus of hostile inquisitors. Marjorie says, "Admit it!" (41), and the limits of the accusation can scarcely be drawn. The phrase applies to every conceivable anxiety. Of course, all of this has been hidden in art as in life by the norms of social conduct: we have been allowed to guess along with Bernice "that Marjorie didn't care" about Warren.

An "eternity" passes, very like a bad dream, and Bernice still can find nothing to say. She now understands the nature of a "suddenly hostile world" (42), which is to say, the world of middle-class democracy perceived by Santayana. From the moment at the beginning when the dance has been described with its watchdogs of social class, one concept has been invoked a number of times, the ritual challenging of individualism. A huge and labored simile takes on the literary work of describing Bernice on the way to her haircut—from Marie Antoinette on the tumbril, to the guillotine with its hangman, to the severed head with its bloody cloth. Bernice too has been reading some books that color her imagination; they occupy nearly a full page in a short story. The invocation means, I think, the fate of distinction in a social world unlikely (as Santayana thought) to uncork the milk of human kindness. At the center is the vital individual, and on the periphery the hostile mass. The figure of Marie Antoinette occurs again—twice in *The Great Gatsby.* Myrtle Wilson (whose apartment has scenes of Versailles) lives in her own *Petit Trianon,* whereas Gatsby's palace has "Marie Antoinette music rooms" (71) that keep her memory in the background of the text.[16]

Psychology and social history are connected. "Bernice Bobs Her Hair" concerns two women who have become familiar over a century of novels. One, a "Saxon princess" (45) with long blond braids and an icy disposition, is social consciousness itself. The other, an outsider, who takes pleasure in feeling the long voluptuous pull of her dark-brown hair as it hangs in a glory far down her back, has less to do with reason and idea. Throughout, Marjorie has been associated with ideas and Bernice with feelings. Marjorie does the work of the conscious mind: she thinks and schemes and deals with life in terms of numbers and conventions; Bernice cries and dreams and falls in love. As far back as the mid-nineteenth century, American writers had been counseled to "present the women in symbolic pairs, blonde and brunette, seraph and sensualist."[17] One of these women has, in Fitzgerald, all of the powers, attractions, and deficiencies of reason. She belongs necessarily to the social world, of which she is mistress. The other belongs in the world of feeling and intuition, dreaming, and the restful dark. At the end, Bernice is part of the night, absorbed into it "swiftly and silently" (46). She is not part of polite civilization but an adversary of it; perhaps she even has some crazy Indian blood in her. We admire her dangerous spirit and know it to be our American own. D. H. Lawrence was soon to state his preference for the symbolism over the social content: "all the other stuff . . . [including] democracy . . . is a sort of by-play."[18] But we might think of it this way: all the other stuff, including democracy, matches up beautifully in a story designed to fit or misfit the individual squarely into her context.

3

"The Diamond" and the Declining West

Early in 1921, while working at *Vanity Fair,* Edmund Wilson wrote to Stanley Dell about the idea of America in current essays and fiction: "The best book I have read lately, and one of the best of modern American novels, is Sinclair Lewis's *Main Street.* You and Marion must read it if you haven't already done so. Lewis has caught the precise tone and mentality of the Middle West; I don't think I should have known how accurate it was if it hadn't been for the Detroiters I was imprisoned with in the army. The theme is much the same as that of *The Age of Innocence.* Think how many remarkable American books have been published in the last year—*Main Street, The Age of Innocence, The Ordeal of Mark Twain,* and Mencken's second series of *Prejudices*—and think how they were all of them written to tell what a terrible place America is".[1]

Wilson was willing to believe that behind these acts of literary hostility was the desire to improve the cultural scene. But he thought that, in spite of everything, things might get worse. Mencken had in *Prejudices* after all, stated a phenomenology of culture unlikely to change: "the plutocracy on top, a vast mass of undifferentiated human blanks bossed by demagogues at the bottom, and a forlorn *intelligentsia* gasping out a precarious life between."[2] The moral and stylistic problems of wealth might well be insoluble.

Later, in a *New Republic* essay (March 15, 1922) Wilson wrote about the difficulty of believing that technology could affect our cultural life. The central problem was the renewal of a nation dominated by the mindless rich. Wilson did not believe that would happen because money and its pursuit dominated Americans: the cities were ugly and the countryside barren. Unlike Europe, there was little respect for ideas. Language itself was a ruin, and "words seem to lie like frame-houses strewn loosely and colorlessly on the unfenced outskirts of a town." Throughout the essay, a wrecked landscape has wider implications: "America, as everyone knows, is not especially beautiful or free. We live and build without taste; our towns are like rubbish-heaps; we abjectly suffer to be stifled; we have not even our original rights; we are a people all alike, uniformly mediocre. . . . the humblest harmony is still an incredible dream. . . . The struggle of reason and art takes on Promethean proportions. It has almost the thrill of the revival of learning at the end of the Middle Ages; a new kind of darkness has whelmed mankind."[3] Wilson adds that intellectuals struggle against the tide of mindless prosperity. The central theme is clear: Now, in 1922, Europe is in decay and so are we, our own hope for squeezing culture out of capitalism having been vanquished.

Decay and decline may come to the imagination of writers of the twenties not from Spengler but from the American landscape—and the west may turn out to be the West—a place that is no longer redemptive. When Wilson reminds his readers of all those "Felix Fays and Carol Kennicotts, reading Man and Superman in remote farms and dreary towns of the vast desert of the West," he implies more than terrain. Fitzgerald was to mention in *The Great Gatsby* (1925) those lost Swede towns of Minnesota and dying Dakota farms that counter the American imagination fixated on progress. In the early twenties writers did not have to read Spengler on decline and fall; they could go directly to Edmund Wilson, to Eliot, to Fitzgerald, and especially to Van Wyck Brooks.[4] After Progressivism, in a book that Wilson thought had provided modern writers with a language of ideas, Brooks had characterized the historical landscape in terms of entropy.[5] He seems purposely to have inverted conventional historical meanings, especially those having to do with progress and the American dream of renewal. Here is a passage that underlies some novels and essays of the twenties. Its title—"Old America"—argues the reversal of a national theme:

> There is a certain spot in New York where I often ruminate in the summer noontime, a lonely, sunny, windy plaza surrounded by ramshackle hoardings and warehouses unfinished and already half in ruin. . . . it is as if one had been suddenly set down in the outskirts of some pioneer city on the plains of the Southwest, one of those half-built cities that sprawl out over the prairie, their long streets hectically alive in the centre but gradually shedding their population and the few poor trees that mitigate the sun's glare, till at last, all but obliterated in alkali dust, they lose themselves in the sand and the silence.
>
> All our towns and cities, I think, have this family likeness and share this alternating aspect of life and death—New York as much as the merest concoction of corrugated iron and clapboards thrown together beside a Western railway to fulfil some fierce evanescent impulse of pioneering enterprise. . . . How many thousand villages, frost-bitten, palsied, full of a morbid, bloodless death-in-life . . . lie scattered across the continent! Even in California, I used to find them on long cross-country walks, villages often enough not half a century old but in a state of essential decay. . . . I suppose it is only natural in the West to find these decayed settlements where time has taken so seriously, as it were, mankind's contempt for permanence. What shocks one is to realize that our Eastern villages, the seats of all the civilization we have, are themselves scarcely anything but the waste and ashes of pioneering.[6]

Brooks, like Wilson, uses landscape to express an idea about national purposes. In so doing he transmits a vast metonym for writers of fiction. (He was not the first to do this and emphatically not the last: Tocqueville anticipated him with an extraordinary description of the ruins of pioneer civilization he had encountered in upstate New York.[7] The idea of the new becoming old powerfully affected Tocqueville, suggesting to him that the American impulse to create anew had from the beginning been compromised and was destined to the same kind of decay as European civilization). For Brooks, a landscape in ruins signifies the original sin of Americanism, its conviction that time can be redeemed through success. It is not only that Nature has been despoiled *but that the original impulse of pioneering was wrong*. We did not, after all, build a civilization; we only ran one down. "A race of pioneers" accomplished only the spoliation of the land and separated itself, finally, from any meaning in cultural life. There never was a "fusion of natural and human elements." Three hundred years of effort had produced only money and wreckage. America has become old without grace or meaning and has produced nothing worth thinking about and very little worth reading.[8] Ruins are ideas for Brooks, and just before the twenties begin, the landscape is the American mind and soul.

The title of Brooks's essay may have been on Fitzgerald's own mind. In 1937 he recalled that "the tortuous death struggle of the old America" had been the subject of his early work.[9] That struggle in Fitzgerald's writing was more subtle and complex than Brooks imagined, however. Fitzgerald clearly has figures who, like Henry C. Gatz and Dan Cody, embody pioneer senility. They have had the brains and spirit leached out of them, have extracted from the land only its crops and ores and put nothing back in. Brooks's description of "the waste and ashes of pioneering" might well be applied to some of Fitzgerald's characters. He provides the fiction of the next decade with an image of that "race of pioneers" who have become "old without pathos, just shabby and bloodless and worn out."[10]

In 1922 that vast metonym of wreckage and wealth was used by Fitzgerald in a more complex way. In "The Diamond As Big As The Ritz" Fitzgerald starts in the Midwest and goes to the far West, but never really leaves the ideological terrain of Wilson and Brooks. Both aspects of the West and of the west are covered: pitiless decay that suggests the senility of American ideas and wealth that is the dominant American fact.

"The Diamond As Big As The Ritz" begins in the Hell of the middle class, a place described by Van Wyck Brooks in 1918 as "The Culture of Industrialism." In Fitzgerald, the best possible business advertisement for Hades might well be "Your Opportunity," whereas in Brooks our national aim is "getting on in the world and getting up in the world." In Fitzgerald, "the simple piety prevalent in Hades has the earnest worship of and respect for riches as the first article of its creed" (186).[11] In the less fluent words of Brooks, we commercialize everything and "associate activity almost solely with material ends." That is because "life itself no longer possesses any other meaning."[12] As for that virtue of "simple piety," the theology of everyday life in "Hades" was neatly handled in 1922 by *Civilization in the United States*. As one of its concluding essays states, "the transposition of ideals from the religious and moral field to the practical and economic, leaves only a very thin ground *for personal piety*."[13] In the early twenties, money and God are easily and often confused. This is how *Civilization in the United States* flatly puts the matter: our captains of industry believe that they are in place, like kings, "by the grace of God."[14] In Fitzgerald, they are in fact "money-kings" (183).

Braddock Washington may not be entirely a megalomaniac.[15] He was certainly not unfamiliar as a representative figure in the first generation of our century. According to H. W. Brands in his 1997 biography, *T. R.: The Last Romantic*, one George Baer had defended the coal trust against reform in a letter stating that its members were "the Christian men to whom God in His infinite wisdom has given the control of the property interests of the country." The appearance of this in print

> provoked a squall of outrage. The New York *Evening Post* called the letter "extraordinary"; the New York *Times* said it seemed to "verge very close upon unconscious blasphemy." The religious press was more incensed still. The Chicago *Standard*, a Baptist paper, castigated "the selfish, ignorant cant that this captain of industry mistakes for religion." An Episcopal paper from New York called Baer's statement "a ghastly blasphemy," while another Baptist journal, from Boston, declared, "the doctrine of the divine right of kings was bad enough, but not so intolerable as the doctrine of the divine right of plutocrats to administer things in general with the presumption that what it pleases them to do is the will of God."[16]

Knowing the "will of God" it is perhaps no wonder that as Fitzgerald put it, they should know also the "price of God." Some of his themes were decidedly in the public realm.

"The Diamond as Big as the Ritz" starts off by mentioning a text that matters more to Americans in the early twenties than the works of Van Wyck Brooks, F. Scott Fitzgerald, and Edmund Wilson combined. To read the *World Almanac* is to be convinced that what matters in American life, even at prep school, is the income and taxation of those "money-kings," especially as measured against the competition of "catch-penny capitalists, financial small-fry, petty merchants and money-lenders" (184). John T. Unger gets two of the best money-culture lines in American literary history: "I like very rich people," and "the richer a fella is, the better I like him" (184). No one in America would be caught dead saying them, but everyone understands them. The lines are stunning, messages from the cultural libido directly to the ego with very little intervention.But it is not entirely a matter of breaking decorums. The *World Almanac* embedded in Fitzgerald's text reminds us of the primal importance of measure and number in American life. Embedded in Fitzgerald's narration, it suggests our grand principle of evaluation.

~

The first section of "The Diamond as Big as the Ritz" ends with a description of the richest man in the world; the second begins by describing the ruins of what once seemed to be the future. The two ideas are connected. We are in the West, in furthest Montana, because it is an idea as well as a place, the wrecked frontier. This is "the village of Fish" (185) for which Brooks had provided a categorical meaning: "it is the American village that most betrays the impulse of our civilization, a civilization that perpetually overreaches itself only to be obliged to surrender again and again to nature everything it has gained."[17] Here, in Brooks, the American enterprise has ended in ruin and silence; whereas in Fitzgerald the ending has been anticipated by the beginning.

"The Diamond As Big As The Ritz," with its wealth of details on the period from the Civil War on, is a revisionist history of what Mencken called "the Gilded Age, the Mauve Decade and the Purple Nineties."[18] It continues into the first decades of the twentieth century, propelled by the energies of Mencken, Brooks, and those others who had pondered the lives of malefactors of great wealth. Well before 1922, Mencken had satirized the style of the leading American plutocrats. His 1918 essay on Rockefeller and Morgan—a modern version of The Use of Riches—had begun with an invitation to his disciples: "On the general stupidity and hunkerousness of millionaires a formidable tome might be written—a job I resign herewith to anyone diligent enough to assemble the facts." Nevertheless, Mencken persisted, arguing that the fundamental difficulty of the millionaire in America was spending his money. Because making money had nothing to do with using it, the millionaire was predestined to be swindled by the arbiters of style and to make a fool of himself by imitating art. J. Pierpont Morgan became a model for any subsequent Midas: He had accumulated the proofs of his magnificence and set about their display, Mencken wrote, like a "Philistine with an unlimited bank account."[19] These ideas about American plutocracy were reprinted in that second volume of *Prejudices* so much admired by Edmund Wilson and that Fitzgerald reviewed.[20]

Mencken's essay on "American Culture" opens with the observation that, without an aristocracy of blood or mind, Americans necessarily worship "dollars" and "diamonds." We may once have had a native aristocracy, which he identifies with "the Virginia of the Eighteenth Century," but "the promise died."[21] As scholarship has recently noted, "the aristocracy of Maryland and Virginia" is important in this story.[22] Mencken describes a plutocracy in the robes of aristocracy, entirely bogus. It wants only to be isolated and (at times Mencken seems to be providing metaphors for fiction) free from attack. It is stupid and superstitious and almost elementally insecure. It is also cruel and full of its own moral certainties. A final point leads us to understand what is missing in Braddock Washington (and in that other fake patrician, Tom Buchanan): "In other countries," Mencken writes, "the plutocracy has often produced men of reflective and analytical habit, eager to rationalize its instincts and to bring it into some sort of relationship to the main streams of human thought." But our denatured plutocracy wants most of all absolute freedom from social criticism, hence Fitzgerald's own *figura* of a palace built near a prison, for "middle-class Americans of the more spirited type."

~

Fitzgerald had been thinking not only about the moral and political problems of money and power but also about the implications of style. And in this story, as in much else, he may be thinking that the very rich really *are* like us. In a world of modernism, Braddock Washington's castle looks like *Neuchwannstein*. Within, it is a teenager's dream of the good life: there are no visible books, and everything looks or smells or tastes good. Fitzgerald, a highly capable allegorist, displays a place in which everything refers itself to the five senses, especially to overwhelmed sight and taste. Satisfaction of the senses is obsessive. Experience is tactile: the bed is like "a cloud" because that is current adspeak. There is an encrypted vocabulary of fake lyric in twenties' magazines about clouds and flowers and gold and diamonds, all of which represent mass-market imaginative excellence. These have become the great unusable metaphors, words without a country, taken over by hacks. John Ungar's clothes are removed by Old Retainers because movie and magazine romances describe high style in the land of silver forks. Bathwater is at body temperature and is mixed with "rosewater" because the harem movies of De Mille and the novels they are based on have for the last few years been retailing such wicked delights. A half-century of dime romances (Nick Carraway will learn to recognize them) has made the consumer familiar with "ebony" panels and other, moral, exotica.

The palace reintroduces Mencken's ideas about the spending problems of millionaires. Everything is "pungent" and "honeyed" and not entirely because the place tends to become temporarily full of teenage guests: this is Braddock Washington's Pemberley, a faithful reflection of the taste and style of American plutocracy. These things, themselves commercialized, are now expressed by marketplace technology. In the following passage, description works in diminuendo, moving from a heroic source of power to its trivialized effect. George F. Babbitt worries at exactly the same time as this story (1922) that some people may "think these mechanical improvements are all that we stand for."[23] He may well be right: "The water turned to a pale rose color and jets of liquid soap spurted into it from four miniature walrus heads at the corners of the bath. In a moment a dozen little paddle-wheels, fixed to the sides, had churned the mixture into a radiant rainbow of pink foam which enveloped him softly with its delicious lightness, and burst in shining, rosy bubbles here and there about him" (191).

There is more to this than wretched excess. In *The New Republic* essay that I have cited (March 15, 1922) Edmund Wilson had already rejected techno-triviality: "Machines are not novelties to me, as they are to Signor Marinetti. I come from the land of machines and have been bored to death by too many of them." We note that Fitzgerald's description has commercial echoes: only advertisement copy now uses "rose" and "pink," which have become the colors of the marketplace, endowing objects with false aesthetic value and ideas with false moral value. By 1925, Wilson had become fascinated by the commercialism of style and its attenuation of meaning. He made a list of some forty current shades of hosiery, guessing ingenuously that the industry "must be employing poets" to come up with them. Among them were, "peach," "pearl," "rose taupe," "blonde satin," "blush," "shell pink," "gold," "rose nutmeg," "peach nude," and "blush pink."[24] Wilson implies the new marketplace artiness; whereas Fitzgerald captures the softness and sweetness and foaminess that delights the masscult mind and its close analogue, the mind of plutocracy. The passage responds to the problem Wilson foresaw: Technology, wealth, and democracy may well unite—but only to produce rose taupe, rose nutmeg, and pink foam.

Most important of all, the issue of technological style becomes that of "the whole moral code" as stated by Walter Lippmann in 1922: "The stereotype represented by such words as 'progress' and 'perfection' was composed fundamentally of mechanical inventions. And mechanical it has remained, on the whole, to this day. In America more than anywhere else, the spectacle of mechanical progress has made so deep an impression, that it has suffused the whole moral code."[25] His ending rightly implies that productivity, perceived through cost, price, and quantity, determines and even becomes morality. Lippmann thought this raised the ante: we were no longer concerned with the deplorable taste of the rich but their translation of American values.

John T. Unger is a chrysalis of the new citizen for whom wealth has become virtue, a figure acidly described in *Public Opinion*. The hugely unsympathetic beginning of Fitzgerald's story establishes John as an ambiguous hero, perhaps no less so than any or all other Americans. He brings to fiction what Lippmann was in the process of bringing to another sector of debate. As Lippmann put the matter, "in the magazines devoted to the religion of success," millionaires displace all others in American history. With this "religion" now so firmly in place there comes inevitably a theology: "victory over mountains, wildernesses, distance, and human competition has even done duty for that part of religious feeling which is a sense of communion with the purpose of the universe."[26] Fitzgerald's story disputes that "victory" over the American landscape, and it translates into highly critical terms any idea of "communion."

The reason that Washington's castle is so stylized *is that the transference noted by Lippmann is already in place.* John T. Unger recognizes in mechanized perfection the good life completed—until certain minor problems about living and dying arise. The action takes place in a philosophical world in which Lippmann or John Dewey might as well never have existed.

Washington's castle, which contains everything that can be ordered, manufactured or consumed, encodes the American economy itself. We know enough to reason not the need, but very little in it is needed. The text refers often to jewels, described in terms of show and costliness—which is to say that the story is full of wealth pretending to be art. In "May Day" (published in Mencken's *Smart Set,* 1920), Fitzgerald had described the transfer from the poetic imagination to the marketplace. Xanadu had become New York, and "the merchants had flocked thither from the South and West with their households to taste of all the luscious feasts and witness the lavish entertainments prepared—and to buy for their women furs against the next winter and bags of golden mesh and varicolored slippers of silk and silver and rose satin and cloth of gold."[27] In fact, as far as the eye can see, there are only buyers and sellers, lenders and borrowers, for trinkets and for lives. As jewels and silver and gold appear in their full-blooded form in the 1922 story, they masquerade as art; but we already know from the 1920 story that they denote marketplace relationships.

In 1921, the year between Fitzgerald's two stories, *Vanity Fair* printed many ad images of rings, bracelets, watches, pendants, and jewels, accompanied by voluminous copy claiming that consumption of these goods raised social status. The March issue's ads celebrated "wonderful workmanship and ingenious mechanism" in precious metals, which made every man a patron if not a magnate; the May issue marketed silver and gold trinkets that endowed the buyer with social classiness; the July issue offered from the magazine's own shopping service an enormous silver gilt radiator cap in the shape of a rooster (it seems to have been about a foot high) "for the large car of dignity and assurance." It makes Gatsby's Rolls or Washington's "station wagon" seem restrained, if not funereal. Advertisement copy argued that by buying anything we could become anything and that anything could be bought.

Our impression of the Washington world is that it is a social order in which class predominates. But it is also an economy, or realm of numbers. Relationships are numerical: Fitz-Norman deals with five emperors, eleven kings and three princes; accumulates a billion in gold, deposits his cash in a thousand bank accounts; promises a temple to be constructed by ten thousand workmen; has Critchtichiello killed fourteen times. Those fourteen separate murders are exaggerations, not deviations: John says that he should himself "marry the daughter of some well-to-do wholesale hardware man from Omaha or Sioux City, and be content with her half-million," an equation in the disguise of an ethic. Throughout the narrative, we read a subtext of universal valuation: "expensive. . . . wealthy. . . . richest. . . . million. . . . income. . . . money. . . . salary. . . . prices. . . . poor. . . . buying. . . . bribe. . . . price. . . . proposition. . . . unlimited amount" (183–213). These terms give the text its basic metaphor of cost and value asserted over essence. Some numbers remain quantitatively but not morally indeterminate: "Why, father and mother have sacrificed some of their best friends just as we have" (205).

The problems in this story have marketplace solutions, and nearly every solution can be quantified. Fitzgerald poses problems that are *least* capable of reduction—the murder of Abel by Cain, the shooting of fourteen different Critchtichiellos—and suggests how money and power free of other considerations might approach them. The castle works on certain principles, most salient, the transfer of economic values to moral issues, from the cost of slaves to that of silence. Human issues are addressed as marketplace decisions. Washington's speech to the prisoners on his estate is contractual, which is why his statement rings true and why it is intelligent: "I've offered to have all or any of you painlessly executed if you wish. I've offered to have your wives, sweethearts, children, and mothers kidnapped and brought out here. I'll enlarge your place down there and feed and clothe you the rest of your lives. If there was some method of producing permanent amnesia I'd have all of you operated on and released immediately" (200).

Washington treats the human realm as if it were the mechanical realm, that is, as part of that new moral code noted by Lippmann in the aptly titled *Public Opinion* of 1922. Lippmann's capitalist and Fitzgerald's both function at exactly the same time; and both move easily from one realm to another—although we would like to think that that is impossible. (By 1929, in *A Preface to Morals,* Lippmann was to develop "the fallacy of the theory of natural liberty," which predicted that freedom may result only in "the supremacy of the acquisitive instinct." One consequence, which we see under the regime of capitalism, is "not a social order at all" but life as marketplace. Anything in it regardless of moral value is feasible).[28]

The passage is a set of propositions requiring answers from its immediate audience. It also requires answers from its readers, who understand the alternatives of affirmation or denial. Yet, before those answers can be provided, a more central question must be addressed: Why is this story a fantasy? Realism had already depicted mindless money with great skill in Mencken, Brooks, Sinclair Lewis—even in the contemporary George Grosz who was busy providing a generation with menacing images of capitalism. In all of these portrayals, the rich suffered from a fundamental lack of imagination. They were simply boors on a larger scale. Braddock Washington, however, does not look like anything imagined by Mencken or drawn by George Grosz. The story has its own internal issues.

What Washington says is shocking, not because it is crazy but because it is reasonable. He is an economic principle disguised as a social principle. As a depiction of the reasoning of wealth, his is a far more interesting solution than that proposed by the Progressives and their followers, who thought plutocracy insufficiently demonic.

4

The Great Gatsby and the Good American Life

F. Scott Fitzgerald wanted to make *The Great Gatsby* the great American novel of his century. He succeeded for certain reasons, among them was his understanding that a new novel required a new mode to be provided by modernism. And he deployed a set of enormously important ideas at a moment when they were being debated by the nation.

The Great Gatsby is often said to be an evolutionary form of Fitzgerald's work, but I think that it is a mutation. He agreed with his friend and critic Edmund Wilson who had encouraged him to forget his earlier writing and move on to new plots, characters, and ideas. In fact, he instructed his editor Max Perkins to have the jacket for his 1926 volume of stories, *All the Sad Young Men,* "show transition from his early exuberant stories of youth which created a new type of American girl and the later and more serious mood which produced *The Great Gatsby* and marked him as one of the half dozen masters of English prose now writing in America"[1]—a nice assessment on both points. There is much in *The Great Gatsby* that does not have a literary history. It is as accurate and self-justifying as a photograph—something often encountered in its pages.

Fitzgerald's choice of place and subject was itself a statement of purpose. H. L. Mencken had in 1924 identified the life of post-war New York City as the natural new subject of the American novel. That life was monied, vulgar, noisy, chaotic, and immoral; hence it was more interesting than anything that could be served up by the literature of gentility. He was fascinated by the same New York crowds that provide the background for Fitzgerald. He too understood their figurative meaning. The frenzied life of Manhattan, its open pursuit of sex, money, and booze was, Mencken wrote, a "spectacle, lush and barbaric in its every detail, [which] offers the material for a great imaginative literature." A new kind of American novel might not only capture the moment but comprehend a new experience in American history, the replacement of Victorian public conscience by modern subjectivity. Mencken told aspiring writers that the New York scene—democracy in its current incarnation—"ought to be far more attractive to novelists than it is."[2]

An enormous amount of the telling of Fitzgerald's story is about New York as well as about Gatsby. The modern moment had after all found its correlative: the great literary and artistic movement of the century's beginnings saw the social world from the urban, dislocated point of view of *The Waste Land*. Modernism provided Fitzgerald, Hemingway, and other writers with not only tactics but also a new sensibility. For example, as Susan Sontag writes of cityscape in photography, "bleak factory buildings and billboard-cluttered avenues look as beautiful, through the camera's eye, as churches and pastoral landscapes. More beautiful, by modern taste."[3] Ezra Pound had written about the aesthetic power of city lights; Hemingway began his description of Paris in *The Sun Also Rises* with its "electric signs"; Blaise Cendrars theorized that billboard-cluttered avenues had for the first time made urban landscape visually interesting. Ordinary things were accepted—welcomed—by modernist writers. They challenged the high seriousness of art and artiness. In *The Great Gatsby* Fitzgerald writes with authority about ads, photos, automobiles, magazines, and Broadway musicals as if these things too fuel the energies of art: "the cars from New York are parked five deep in the drive, and already the halls and salons and verandas are gaudy with primary colors and hair shorn in strange new ways and shawls beyond the dreams of Castile" (34).[4] Production, entertainment, style, and consumption are native subjects of modernism, often displacing what is merely natural. In the case of a certain billboard featuring Doctor T. J. Eckleburg—both symbol and sign of the times—they become part of the weave of a great American novel.

Like any other intellectual movement, modernism had its sacred texts. From its use of Baudelaire to that of T. S. Eliot it was self-referential. *The Great Gatsby* calls attention to its intellectual allegiances, and as Robert Emmet Long has observed, Fitzgerald brings the plot and idealistic idea of *Almayer's Folly* up to date: A young adventurer falls in love, at first succeeds, then loses everything.[5] New ideas of form are displayed, and throughout Fitzgerald's deeply symbolic novel, we become aware of how far we have gone from the values of realism. As for subject, Mencken may have wanted a Great American Novel on social life in New York, but when it came out, he did not recognize it. I think he expected something that might have been called *Prohibition on Broadway.* He did not expect a romance or a myth as powerful as that of *The Waste Land*—what Nick Carraway calls a quest for the grail. As for style, Fitzgerald's novel of New York is nowhere more modernist than in its impressionism. Expecting hard-edged delineation of the manners and mores of the Jazz Age, we find instead evocations of yellow cocktail music and trembling opal and a moon produced out of a caterer's basket. The Jazz Age is there, but the story is its own telling.

Fitzgerald's characters are more than the sum of their own experiences: they constitute America itself as it moves into the Jazz Age. A larger story swirls around them, however, and its meaning is suggested by an early, unused title for the novel: *Under the Red, White, and Blue.*

The Great Gatsby reflects national issues. Just before Fitzgerald came of age, Walter Lippmann had stated that "those who are young to-day are born into a world in which the foundations of the older order survive only as habits or by default." And soon after the publication of *The Great Gatsby,* John Dewey was to write that "the loyalties which once held individuals, which gave them support, direction, and unity of outlook on life, have well-nigh disappeared."[6] *The Great Gatsby* shows a version of the new social world criticized by the Public Philosophy that Lippmann and Dewey represented. It is a world of broken relationships and false relationships, a world of money and success rather than of social responsibility, a world in which individuals are all too free to determine their moral destinies. Daisy warns Nick and the reader about this world when she says, in the first chapter, "I think everything's terrible anyhow" (17). Because she believes that, she is free to act any way she wants.

One issue of the novel is loyalty to love, another is loyalty to friendship. Nick himself exemplifies loyalty to people and ideas, whereas Daisy and Tom have freed themselves from troublesome conscience—and from even more troublesome self-awareness. They will be loyal neither to idea nor person. They have no significant sense of self to which they can be true. Important referents are involved, because Americans had for some time been advised of the perilous subjectivity of their lives and the absence of will. The Public Philosophy often called the nation to account for the way it made and spent money, about its class relationships, about the state of our national character. Here is how Josiah Royce described American uncertainties a year or two before Fitzgerald went to Princeton: "Since the war, our transformed and restless people has been seeking not only for religious, but for moral guidance. What are the principles that can show us the course to follow in the often pathless wilderness of the new democracy? It frequently seems as if, in every crisis of our greater social affairs, we needed somebody to tell us both our dream and the interpretation thereof. We are eager to have life. . . . But what life?"[7] Readers who now come to Fitzgerald's novel and to the twenties are inclined to think that the oft-mentioned subject of the American Dream is a matter of personal freedom and financial success; however, writers like Royce and Lippmann described the dream in different terms. They related it to the building of the nation in the eighteenth century and to the qualities of character that nation building implied. They also suggested that it was disappearing into history.

Perhaps it was already gone. Were there even models left for us to understand? Milton R. Stern agrees in *The Golden Moment* that the possibility of even *understanding* the dream had disappeared. Here is how he describes a central problem in Fitzgerald's novel: "The poor, naive, believing son of a bitch. He dreamed of a country in the mind and he got East and West Egg. He dreamed of a future magic self and he got the history of Dan Cody. He dreamed of a life of unlimited possibility and he got Hopalong Cassidy, Horatio Alger, and Ben Franklin's 'The Way to Wealth.' What else could he imitate?"[8] Gatsby is a hero in a world without heroism, unable to connect "with the past and the eternities."[9]

For Fitzgerald himself the dream was quite literally about the vanishing quality of greatness. It meant displaying in private life those daring unselfish qualities that had made America possible. This was a subject on Fitzgerald's mind in the twenties. We are fortunate that he defined it in the conclusion of his short story "The Swimmers" (1929)[10]: "France was a land, England was a people, but America, having about it still that quality of the idea, was harder to utter—it was the graves at Shiloh and the tired, drawn, nervous faces of its great men, and the country boys dying in the Argonne for a phrase that was empty before their bodies withered. It was a willingness of the heart" (512). It would be difficult to understand *The Great Gatsby* without that last line. Nevertheless, as good as that line is, it is not entirely original. It comes from a good deal of reading about the nation. Harold E. Stearns, one of the most thoughtful critics of Americanism in the early twenties, identified "willingness" as "the old and traditional American" style of spiritual generosity in a material world. If affirmed character and will, resisting what seemed to be unalterable "economic and social forces." "Willingness" was, according to Stearns, part (and the best part) of our national character.[11] It was clearly a form of greatness, part of the reason why Gatsby is the Great Gatsby.

First, however, we must examine the opposite of this idea of greatness: Against Royce's panoramic vision of national development, responsibility, and obligation, a character like that of Tom Buchanan is a compendium of American failures. He is rich with no conscience, moralistic without being moral, exclusionary, racist, and, above all, untrue to any self-conception. He is Royce's nightmare and the nightmare of the Public Philosophy, a figure of resentment and of absolute, solipsistic subjectivity.

How is Gatsby himself to be measured? The values that Fitzgerald recalled from the years before the Jazz Age did not consist wholly of moral prohibitions, although clearly they derive from a traditional morality "based upon spirit over matter."[12] William James did indeed preach fully conscious responsibility for our moral decisions; George Santayana did lecture the American public about its responsibility to create a meaningful social order; and John Dewey did repeatedly outline the conditions for an informed public adapting to necessary social change. But more was implied than these things. James, in a letter to H. G. Wells that has become part of our intellectual history, remarked on the new and alarming "worship of the bitch-goddess SUCCESS" in America.[13] He saw that prosperity and power might in themselves become trivial and boring. Life demanded intense powers of imagination, even romantic love and devotion. He argued for dedication to people and ideas and against the state of mind that lost itself in meaningless subjectivity, which would prove to be a form of unconsciousness not simply metaphorical. Life demanded goals, sacrifice, and a certain amount of risk. In fact, James once wondered idly if the last heroes in America might not be outside the law, choosing *not* to be prudentially middle-class. So far as James could see, there was nothing wrong (excess and ignorance apart) in emotional dedication to a cause. The characters of *The Great Gatsby* enact many a drama scripted by American philosophy, and its language mirrors the language of debate about a country becoming ever more monied and less heroic, less true—except for Jay Gatsby—to the grand passions of its past.

Gatsby has the capacity for the pursuit of happiness. He believes in his dream and in Daisy as its object. He has a passion for belief, and although he may be wrong about the kind of happiness that is possible and about the woman who represents that happiness, he has committed himself to the dream. Gatsby's pursuit of Daisy against impossible odds is perhaps the final form of the American will to wring a new life from destiny.

Of course, Gatsby is imperfect. In spite of his idealism, his idea of the good life seems merely to be the acquisition of money, things, property. Possibly the most famous literary possession of our century is his car in "a rich cream color, bright with nickel, swollen here and there in its monstrous length with triumphant hatboxes and supper-boxes and tool-boxes, and terraced with a labyrinth of wind-shields that mirrored a dozen suns" (51). In this book we tend to see the sun as it is reflected by produced things. Gatsby's house (like Myrtle's apartment) is a showcase of consumption. Nevertheless, an enormously shrewd essay by Santayana in 1920 (its title, fittingly, is "Materialism and Idealism in American Life") had pointed out that one of these quantities did not necessarily cancel out the other. Gatsby is materialistic because Americans do not have many other alternatives. Material life offers one of the few recognized ways in which the American can *express* his idealism. This is how Santayana describes the issue:

> For the American the urgency of his novel attack upon matter, his zeal in gathering its fruits, precludes meanderings in primrose paths; devices must be short cuts. . . . There is an enthusiasm in his sympathetic handling of material forces which goes far to cancel the illiberal character which it might otherwise assume. . . . his ideals fall into the form of premonitions and prophecies; and his studious prophecies often come true. So do the happy workmanlike ideals of the American. When a poor boy, perhaps, he dreams of an education, and presently he gets an education, or at least a degree; he dreams of growing rich, and he grows rich. . . . He dreams of helping to carry on and to accelerate the movement of a vast, seething progressive society, and he actually does so. Ideals clinging so close to nature are almost sure of fulfillment; the American beams with a certain self-confidence and sense of mastery; he feels that God and nature are working with him.[14]

Money, after all, has been only a means to express otherwise inchoate ideas. Santayana, famously, was convinced that this was a kind of secular theology, which suggests one way to approach Jay Gatsby's own ideas. One of the central themes of Fitzgerald's novel is the application of religious feeling to secular experience; one of the central themes of Santayana is the representativeness of this American conception.

What are the obstacles to Gatsby's dream, apart from intractable human nature, time, and chance? Gatsby does not want only to be a success, he wants to be a gentleman. Meyer Wolfshiem reminds us several times that he has fulfilled *both* of his desires, but Wolfshiem turns out to be less than a reliable judge. One of the most important things for readers at our end of the century to remember is that democratic life was different in 1922. Throughout Fitzgerald's novels and stories we see aspiration meeting rejection. The text refers to a democracy that current readers may not recognize. Nick, Wolfshiem, Tom, and even Myrtle Wilson have an ideal social type in mind. So does Gatsby.

We might be disposed to think that, especially in America, a self-made man would be proud of his achievement. But Gatsby hides his past—although it has been interesting enough to have provided the material for a dozen novels. He begins life on a worked-out farm, learns how to read and think with not much help, goes on his *wahnderjahre,* becomes irresistible to women, rescues a yacht from disaster, tops it all off by becoming (Basil Duke Lee dreams of this) a gentleman criminal. If this reminds us of famous lives and books, it is intended to. Every literary-biographical theme we can imagine has been part of his forgotten life: there are echoes of David Copperfield, Julien Sorel, Compton Mackenzie, Horatio Alger, Joseph Conrad, and even Raffles, the suave society crook admired by Fitzgerald and also by George Orwell when they were schoolboys. But this adventurous story remains profoundly uninteresting to Gatsby, although it fascinates Nick.

Gatsby does not want to be praised for what he is, but for what he is not. In this, he represents the tensions of the early twenties. Wolfshiem, who respects social standards (admittedly from a distance), thinks about Gatsby being "a perfect gentleman" and "a man of fine breeding" (57). Myrtle Wilson has married her husband George "because I thought he was a gentleman." She pumps gas, but says the same thing as Wolfshiem about the ideal social type: "I thought he knew something about breeding" (30). Her friend Lucille McKee, who is by no means Mrs. Astor, has dropped a suitor, she says, because "he was way below" (29) her. Even Tom Buchanan, with his delusions of science and art and all that, wants badly to assert patrician responsibility and to assert the values of his social class.

When Gatsby says, "Here's another thing I always carry" (53), it is final proof that his early life has disappeared, a photo of "Oxford days" showing that he has always belonged, so to speak, among his peers. Gatsby is not only the leading man of the Jazz Age but the last great figure of the gentleman hero. He understands and accepts that inequality is characteristic of his democratic moment. Such inequality is unfair, but there is a benefit: his character is thickened, made more intense, by obsolete qualities of courtesy, thoughtfulness, and honor. Whether dealing with Nick Carraway or Daisy or a girl who has torn her gown at his party, he has that nobility unknown to West Egg, forgotten by East Egg and by our national memory. The irony of the novel is that he has become far more of a gentleman than his social adversaries—"the whole damn bunch" (120) of them.

Before *The Great Gatsby,* Fitzgerald dealt with the educated and literate world. He told us possibly more than we want to know about the privileged life of Princeton and its college-boy weekends in Manhattan. The creation of Jimmy Gatz, Myrtle Wilson, and George Wilson shows how far his understanding developed. In his correspondence with Max Perkins, his editor at Scribner's, Fitzgerald went so far as to state that Myrtle Wilson was a more achieved character than Daisy Fay Buchanan. There are reasons for that: Daisy and Gatsby do not have the same hard delineation as their surrounding cast. They are partly mythical and even allegorical. Myrtle belongs to the everyday world. Fitzgerald's tactic in establishing her is to describe in detail her relationship to that world and to allow her to reveal her taste and style. Daisy, rarely described directly, is part idea; Myrtle, often described directly, is understood through her countless acquisitions. Her apartment has as much to say about her conception of herself as Gatsby's palace has to say about his:

> The apartment was on the top floor—a small living room, a small dining room, a small bedroom and a bath. The living room was crowded to the doors with a set of tapestried furniture entirely too large for it so that to move about was to stumble continually over scenes of ladies swinging in the gardens of Versailles. . . . Several old copies of "Town Tattle" lay on the table together with a copy of "Simon called Peter" and some of the small scandal magazines of Broadway. Mrs. Wilson was first concerned with the dog. A reluctant elevator boy went for a box full of straw and some milk to which he added on his own initiative a tin of large hard dog biscuits—one of which decomposed apathetically in the saucer of milk all afternoon. (25)

When we see Myrtle's arrangements we see the inside of her mind. There are many things that are admirable about her, but, like Gatsby, she has never understood essential models of style. He wants to be a gentleman; she wants to be a lady: what are the odds? Myrtle, who is blue-collar, has surrounded herself with the artifacts of the middle class. She does not understand even these things very well, which argues that her understanding of Tom (who exists many levels above the middle class) is itself deficient. Everything about the apartment suggests that Myrtle, like Gatsby, has gotten her ideas about style and class from the mass market. Not only are the magazines and books in plain sight, the furnishings are a demonstration of what she has learned from newsstand culture.

There are more objects and things described in this apartment than the mind can easily register. Myrtle has tried to *accumulate* her social character. She has bought the tapestries because they provide her self-image, more grandiose than we might guess at first sight, when all she seems to have is carnal intelligence. She has bought books, magazines, furniture, pictures, and "police dog" because of the urgings of advertisements that promise status through acquisition. Her catalogue of all the things she's "got to get" (31) —a massage, a wave, a collar for the dog, a wreath, an ash tray—is a blueprint for becoming what that she knows she is not. But as Stern suggests, even the possibilities of imitation have diminished. That phrase "small," repeated four times in a paragraph, says something about great expectations compressed into limited psychological space.

Beneath the skin of the novel is a powerful opposition between the language of navigation and will, of drift and unconsciousness. That opposition comes, I think, from discourse of the Public Philosophy.[15] Vital energy, for example, implies strength of character. That energy in Jay Gatsby, in Myrtle Wilson and, from time to time, in Nick Carraway suggests the ability to lead a life of feeling. It states the intensity and emotional commitment that are so rare among others in this story. So, when we see Gatsby at rest—as near to rest as he gets—we see his *American* readiness for experience: "He was balancing himself on the dashboard of his car with that resourcefulness of movement that is so peculiarly American—that comes, I suppose, with the absence of lifting work or rigid sitting in youth and, even more, with the formless grace of our nervous, sporadic games. This quality was continually breaking through his punctilious manner in the shape of restlessness. He was never quite still; there was always a tapping foot somewhere or the impatient opening and closing of a hand" (51). "Vitality," "energy," and the "restlessness" that Gatsby displays are common phrases of the early twentieth century. Such phrases are shorthand (as in the speeches and writings of Teddy Roosevelt), for American creative possibility. Always in motion, Gatsby is intended to remind us of qualities praised not only by novelists but also by those who believed that in order to have a moral life one had first to have great energy, concentrated will, and high resolution. Against the language of this passage we need to poise the language describing others in the text. They are (except for Jordan's ungoverned will) sensed through terms of indolence, inertia, withdrawal, and even paralysis. Daisy Fay Buchanan's languor—"What do people plan?" (13)—shows the life of the Lotos-eaters. Even Jordan becomes not only situationally "bored" but existentially; and she is, of course, too wise or, like Daisy, perhaps too "sophisticated" to dream at all. Background figures are sick, silent, "lethargic," or paralytically drunk.

Tom and Daisy lead quintessentially unexamined lives. As Nick puts it, they act and seem to live "for no particular reason" (9)—anathema to the philosophy of vital energy. That phrase "drift," used repeatedly in the opening of *The Great Gatsby,* reminds Fitzgerald's readers of American debates very much unfinished: I have mentioned Lippmann, who had recently written of America as a "nation of uncritical drifters," mindless and self-absorbed.[16] There were political implications, for he concluded that a democracy so diminished might not survive or deserve to survive. On the personal scale, a fatal lack of moral tension is necessarily implied: Fitzgerald's allusive descriptions tell us, a long time before Tom and Daisy and Jordan ever make decisions, how those decisions are likely to be made.

The people at both of Gatsby's parties (and at Myrtle's dissolvent party also) represent "New York," a place but also an idea. "New York" is itself problematic, it being widely understood in the twenties that the city was no longer white, native, or Christian. In fact, according to Charles Merz, "the most fundamental charge being brought by its critics against New York is the charge that here is an 'alien' city, literally un-American and anti-American in its make-up. . . . the city has gone foreign."[17] That is one of the reasons why the language of the novel applied to the life of New York is "tumultuous" and chaotic and why the air is alive with dissonant sounds unheard in the provinces. New York names are among these dissonant sounds, rejecting both familiarity and iambic pentameter. In addition, Meyer Wolfshiem, Gulick, Eckhaust, and Beluga the tobacco importer are objects of suspicion both to Tom Buchanan and to the framers of the Immigration Bill of 1924, the year of the novel's composition. The splendidly mixed and unbalanced procession of names that begins Fitzgerald's fourth chapter implies the uneasy presence in America of those who have come (all too recently) from the wrong parts of Europe. In Manhattan, Nick and Jordan hear that "foreign clamor on the sidewalk" (106), which has made everyone uneasy. It is in the course of things that "Gatz" from *Mitteleuropa* should become the mellifluous, anglophone "Gatsby." Lily Shiel (Fitzgerald's Jewish-Cockney lover, with a name difficult to scan) becomes Sheilah Graham, metrically socially a happier choice.

Breakdown is characteristic of the story and also of its language. We begin with harmonic, rhythmic statement, with long, assured and sweeping sentences, with language that easily imitates music: "And so with the sunshine and the great bursts of leaves growing on the trees" (7). But both story and language move inexorably from harmony to chaos. Starting with the sober, careful, and practiced enunciations of Jay Gatsby we go to another mode that dominates the later telling and experiencing of the story. The language moves from rhythmic precision of statement to cacophony as the narrative moves from day to night and from the description of dreams to that of nightmares.

Fitzgerald opposes harmony and dissonance in both literal and figurative forms, just as he does drift and its mastery. By the end of Gatsby's first party, "most of the remaining women were now having fights with men said to be their husbands" (42). One particular song ends in "gasping broken sobs" (42), and we exit to a "bizarre and tumultuous scene" of collision amid the "harsh discordant din" of auto horns (44). Those "caterwauling horns" are in themselves allusions. Amanda Vaill has recently written that this particular kind of dissonance was in the modernist domain by mid-twenties: Fitzgerald's friend Gerald Murphy collaborated with Fernand Léger in a film of *Ballet mécanique* that featured the sound of machinery, including the "automobile horn."[18] (The original score by George Antheil, played in Paris in 1924, featured among other sounds that of an electric fan disguised as an airplane propeller and also a "battery of cacophones." Aaron Copeland witnessed the performance and thought that it "outsacked the *Sacre,*" which had until then set the international standard for modernist polemic dissonance).[19] The discordant sounds of the film's uncaring mechanical "moving objects" were intended to imply not only human experience in cities but also the meaning of lives in them. There was a great deal of musical dissonance in the first quarter of the new century. The opposition of harmony and disorder was especially useful to modernism, with atonality being understood as "a critique of society" as well as a description of it.[20] Stravinsky invoked the sewing-machine, Honegger the locomotive, and Antheil the machine-gun. The object was, Stravinsky said, that of "producing noise" that characterized the way we live now, and what our lives meant.[21] On this, Eliot was definitive: "the scream of the motor-horn, the rattle of machinery, the grind of wheels" are both facts and symbols "of modern life."[22] Closer to home, Jelly Roll Morton's *Sidewalk Blues* (recorded for Victor in 1926) starts off with a blaring automobile horn, which is a way of letting us know existentially as well as musically where we are. Nick Carraway realizes that the "many-keyed commotion" (81) at Gatsby's second party has explicit social meaning: Daisy hears it and intuitively understands the danger it poses to the soft rhythms of her unconsidered life. In terms of music, what follows is a parable out of Mahler and Schoenberg. Dissonance becomes a trope of social disorder, a warning about fate—and always a reminder of the allusive tactics of modernism.

5

"The Killers" or the Way Things Really Are

According to Kenneth S. Lynn's biography of Hemingway, "behind 'The Killers' lay some obvious influences: Hemingway's firsthand acquaintance with petty criminals in Kansas City, his close observation of the men entering the back room in the Venice Café and the steady attention he paid in the twenties to journalistic accounts, in European as well as American newspapers, of the blood-drenched careers of Chicago hoodlums."[1] Behind the story also is Hemingway's acquaintance by 1926 with vaudeville and with the idea of vaudeville. The connection has long been noted: in 1959 Cleanth Brooks and Robert Penn Warren mentioned the "vaudeville team" of Max and Al and the "gag" and "dialogue" that remind the reader of their "unreal and theatrical quality."[2] The essay is, however, only the briefest of sketches on the subject.

By the mid-1920s, entertainment had become part of visual and literary art. Music hall scores echoed in the work of T. S. Eliot; the lyrics of Broadway hits were reprinted on the pages of F. Scott Fitzgerald; revues and Follies were described in fascinated detail in the essays of Edmund Wilson. *The Waste Land* has in it lyrics from a popular ballad about Mrs. Porter ("a Cairo brothel-keeper, together with her daughter . . . notorious among Australian troops for passing on venereal disease"), which had been set to the tune of Thurland Chattaway's *Red Wing* of 1907.[3] Ruth Prigozy has shown that Broadway songs were important to F. Scott Fitzgerald, who referred in his writings to Libby Holman, Glenn Miller, Paul Whiteman, Benny Goodman, Irving Berlin,

Jerome Kern, and Vincent Youmans.[4] The phrase "the seven lively arts," coined by Gilbert Seldes, was meant to include comics, dancers and Krazy Kat—and to displace such bourgeois delights as grand opera. It was the fate of one of those lively arts, vaudeville, to wax and wane with modernism.

In order to be useful to Hemingway as a subject in 1926, two things had had to happen to vaudeville: the first was its permeation of the social world, the second, its recognition by the intellectual world. We know that the first of these things happened because, from W. C. Fields to Eddie Cantor and even to Ed Sullivan, vaudevillians not only dominated the Palace and the Ziegfeld Follies—hence the imagination of much of New York—they also went on to radio and the movies. The second of these things was a necessary consequence of the first. Here is a brief chronology: In 1922 Mary Cass Canfield wrote of vaudeville (in the *New Republic*) that it need not apologize for comparisons with Robinson and Frost, Masters and Sandburg. In fact, she thought it held its own with the work of Mark Twain as a kind of artistic reaction to our native social repressiveness: "Grotesque or not, vaudeville represents a throwing away of self-consciousness, of Plymouth Rock caution, devoutly to be wished for. Here we countenance the extreme, we encourage idiosyncracy. The dancer or comedian is, sometimes literally, egged on to develop originality; he is adored, never crucified for difference. Miss Fannie Brice and Sir Harry Lauder are examples of vaudeville performers who have been hailed, joyfully and rightfully, as vessels containing the sacred fire, and who have been encouraged into self-emphasis by their audiences."[5] Equally important was the fact of universal intellectual acceptance: "Darius Milhaud, George Auric and the others, write ballets and symphonies in which may be heard the irresponsible 'cancan' of ragtime. John Alden Carpenter, perhaps the most vivid talent among our own composers, will occasionally shift from cooly subtle disharmonies, illustrating poetic or lyric subjects, to write a Krazy Kat Ballet."[6] Vaudeville was for the intellectual world equal to other forms of artistic composition, and it seemed to gain meaning when it was compared to the modes of modernism.

Throughout 1923, Edmund Wilson produced a barrage of pieces on vaudeville ideas and personalities, and on the meaning of dance, jazz, comic scripts, and revues. He identified some of the leading comics and mimes, among them Bert Savoy, Johnny Hudgins, and Bert Williams. He speculated on the satire of vaudeville and especially on its urban modernist meanings. Wilson thought that the Ziegfeld Follies were inherently part of his and Fitzgerald's literary world: "Among those green peacocks and gilded panels, in the luxurious haze of the New Amsterdam, there is realized a glittering vision which rises straight out of the soul of New York. The Follies is such fantasy, such harlequinade as the busy well-to-do New Yorker has been able to make of his life. Expensive, punctual, stiff, it moves with the speed of an express train. It has in it something of Riverside Drive, of the Plaza, of Scott Fitzgerald's novels."[7]

Not for the last time, Wilson thought of vaudeville as an equivalent of Dada. He was especially attuned to vaudeville's depiction of anxiety, writing about Bert Williams as a kind of walking Freudian dream, finding Eddie Cantor and Gilda Gray to be mental incarnations of New York "in terms of entertainment." They expressed the city's "nervous intensity to the tune of harsh and complicated harmonies." He thought that Bert Savoy, an impersonator, was an exceptionally able critic of the styles and aspirations of upper-middle-class Manhattan life.[8] Wilson thought, finally, that vaudeville was a modernist urban art, full of reflections of current experience. He was especially aware of its staccato delivery and its own self-conscious sense of authorship: in Wilson's canon, Bert Savoy mattered as much as any textualized idea.

In 1924 Seldes, a friend of Wilson's and known to both Fitzgerald and Hemingway, published *The Seven Lively Arts*. It was reviewed by Wilson. This book gave intellectuals much to think about. Aside from cataloguing the great and the good performers, it moved into the heady realms of modernist theory. Wilson thought that the book was chaotic, sometimes out of control, and he was right. But Seldes made some important points for the writers who came after him. He did not originate the argument that Chaplin and other comics belonged with Joyce and Eliot (Eliot himself made that point), but he argued consistently that the "lively" arts belonged with so-called higher forms of visual and textual arts.[9] He thought that Broadway comedians like Bert Savoy and George Monroe created stage characters comparable to, say, Mrs. Gamp in Dickens.[10] Most important, at least as far as Hemingway is concerned, was the series of manifestos with which the book ended. Seldes provided an enormous amount of material to anyone inclined to think that conventional American values—and the writings exemplifying them—were bogus.

Seldes took certain modernist beliefs about the unwinding of respectable culture and restated them in terms of comedy, jazz, and even cartoons. For example, Ring Lardner and Mr. Dooley are "more important than James B. Cabell and Joseph Hergesheimer" because they say more about present attitudes toward the present moment. This may now be self-evident, but even Mencken, full of pieties for the groaning earnestness of realism, resisted such ideas. Seldes thought that Florenz Ziegfeld was better than David Belasco and that the circus was better than grand opera.[11] Edmund Wilson thought the last was an exaggeration—but Hemingway might have found the thought more than casually amusing.

It will be useful to cite the last three of Seldes's principles of art high and low, which appear after a number of T. S. Eliot's own remarks on the same subjects in the *Dial:*

> That there exists a "genteel tradition" about the arts which has prevented any just appreciation of the popular arts, and that these have therefore missed the corrective criticism given to the serious arts, receiving instead only abuse.
>
> That therefore the pretentious intellectual is as much responsible as any one for what is actually absurd and vulgar in the lively arts.
>
> That the simple practitioners and simple admirers of the lively arts being uncorrupted by the bogus preserve a sure instinct for what is artistic in America.[12]

Hugh Kenner points out that Eliot's 1920–22 essays in the *Dial* satirize the "official English literary stupidity and dullness" of current fiction and drama while praising shows at The Palladium. (Among Eliot's works is a highly appreciative obituary for a comedienne, Marie Lloyd). So far as he was concerned, music-hall turns—song, drama, and especially comedy—had more life and real "art" in them than anything apt to be supported by polite "Society." And Eliot called attention more than once to the importance of "the music-hall comedian."[13] Perhaps the best account of culture high and low is Wilson's long review of 1924 in which he placed Seldes within "America's new orientation" of ideas begun by Van Wyck Brooks in 1915. Wilson thought that the Seldes book had identified an important strand of modernism. The "inconsecutive" and even "pointless" comic art of vaudevillians like Joe Cook, Charlie Case, and James J. Morton could be compared to Jean Cocteau and understood as a parallel to Dada. He thought it important for readers to realize that the art of vaudeville was above all an accurate response to the post-war world and "the bewildering confusion of the modern city." The disconnected, "pointless," and often resentful vaudeville script shows the way the world is and the way our "*own minds are beginning to work.*"[14]

Finally, in 1925, a year before the writing of "The Killers," an article appeared in *The Drama* on the subject of "The Vaudeville Philosopher" (which may be the right category for Max and Al). It decried the new sensibility of national *ressentiment:*

> There are certain standard subjects that are used almost every night on vaudeville stages through the country. An audience, composed of many persons mentally fatigued after a day's work, learns a philosophy that embraces such precepts as: marriage is an unfortunate institution to which the majority of us resign ourselves; women are fashion-crazy, spend money heedlessly and believe that their husbands are fools; politics is all bunk, Prohibition should be prohibited. . . . marital infidelity is widespread; clandestine affairs of most any sort between at least one married person and another of the opposite sex are comical; and finally "nothing in life really matters. The main thing to do is get all the money you can and keep your mother-in-law as far off as possible."[15]

A few years later, writing about the social mood of the mid-twenties, Fitzgerald described "a wide-spread neurosis" and a significant change in American character. He ascribed the change to the boom, not the bust.[16] Vaudeville seems to have picked up the various kinds of national resentments—many of them in the world of ideas.

To some extent this kind of "philosophy" had always been there because of the daily collision on stage between comic values and what Fitzgerald and others described as our "Victorian" social habit of hypocrisy. Modernism aside, before and during the Great War the national cultural audience had signified a great deal about its sensibility. Willie Hammerstein's Victoria Theatre consciously changed the sentimentality of the music hall. It featured hard-edged discourse on the conflicts of domestic life. It fed off events reported by newspapers and had a symbiotic relationship with them. At the Victoria, comedy was generated out of class, marital and racial conflict, unrepressed anger and anxieties, current "sexual scandals . . . and suffragists."[17] Hammerstein's Victoria had put "newsmakers" on its stage— chorus girls with very public private lives, speech-making suffragettes, and the occasional celebrities who fired shots at their lovers. This is how Joe Laurie Jr. describes Hammerstein's pursuit of the new public consciousness: "he played the killers and near killers."[18]

As early as 1914, the public had become accustomed to seeing the connection between social resentment and theatrical aggression. By the twenties, vaudeville had become increasingly associated with the techniques and values of modernism. Edmund Wilson and Gilbert Seldes among others emphasized the values of non-textual and impermanent arts.[19] As Wilson put the matter two decades later, these were better than "our respectable arts." The new icons of culture—Joe Cook, Charlie Chaplin, Florenz Ziegfeld, Ring Lardner, Krazy Kat, Al Jolson, and Irving Berlin—had an important role in "the liquidation of genteel culture."[20] Vaudeville was a concurrent form of intellectual style. Hemingway came to the subject in mid-decade with a well-defined map of "culture" and of the ways in which comic representation looked at the unrealities of real life.

When Max and Al walk into Henry's lunchroom they are in a confined, lighted, and stagy space with doors for exits and entrances. A running gag begins about not knowing what they want; the gag is at this point merely absurd. Max and Al keep asking each other questions as they go through the formalities of what vaudeville historians call "The

Two-man Act." This "was usually the comedy standout of the bill" because "talking routines" had taken precedence over song, dance, acrobatics and other forms of insurance for comedians. Hemingway follows one specific vaude tradition: "usually it was a straight man with a Hebrew comic."[21] Max is gentile, Al, who could only have come from a kosher convent, is not. The key, however, is that they really are what they are.

Two-man acts were relentlessly ethnic and aggressive beyond anything dreamed today. Done by Olsen & Johnson or Smith & Dale or Weber & Fields they did "The Merry Wop," "The Sport and the Jew," or "Irish by Name but Coons by Birth." The scripts that remain indicate that no punch was pulled, no insult spared. As vaudeville developed, insult gave way to wit. Slapstick was dropped: beginning with belly-laughs, the two-man act after the turn of century utilized "more rational stuff." The costume and demeanor of modern comics indicated a new sophistication, hence the displacement of red noses, checkered coats, and circus shoes by good suits, ties, and stock collars. The two-man act often wore (Hemingway noticed this) city-slicker gray derbies.[22] The act developed "routines" that were highly verbal, demanding interpretation.

The straight man had the most status—he was sane in a world of eccentrics—and he had some pretensions to ideas, education, and even style. Both Max and Al like to play the straight man, and they alternate in the role. When they first enter, the dialogue is unfocused because they are free-wheeling, commenting ad lib on the clock and menu. But they are strangely aggressive and bring into the story attitudes that the story itself does not account for. Some of these attitudes are (so to speak) professional, but others have to do with the genre. All straight men know that the world is composed largely of fools who must be suffered.

Here are two parallel scripts for an opening gag. The first is from Hemingway:

> "This is a hot town," said the other. "What do they call it?"
> "Summit."
> "Ever hear of it?" Al asked his friend.
> "No," said the friend.
> "What do you do here nights?" Al asked.

> "They eat the dinner," his friend said. "They all come here and eat the big dinner."[23] (280)

The second passage suggests that Hemingway has borrowed liberally from vaudeville lore. Scripts that were older than he, provided him with one of his central themes: urban sophistication poised against rural idiocy. A "well-dressed" man (he is in fact an actor) from the big city meets one of the local rubes:

> "What's the name of this town?"
> [. . . . .]
> "Centertown."
> "Where is the theatre?"
> "I don't know," says the native.
> Then the actor looks at him as though he were an idiot.[24]

Hemingway has appropriated the rube's line about not knowing much; he will reverse it, make it into a problem of philosophy. He has exaggerated the free-floating resentment and aggression of comedy, making that the essence of his story.

Max and Al do not like bright boys; the phrase is repeated more than any other in the story. In one of the two-man acts, "The Sport and the Jew," the straight man says to Cohen (whose name has a certain resonance in Hemingway), "You're a pretty smart fellow."[25] He means the opposite. Al and Max are gangsters, satirists, philosophers, and vaudes, but they are above all ironists.[26] Almost everything they say means its opposite, and one of the great resentments in their dialogue is intellectual. The dialogue is economical to a degree—minimalist—but does even more than it seems to do, conveying the meaning not only of statement but also of predisposition.

Max and Al enter the text with attitudes about a number of things. As professionals, they have ideas about the job, but as comedians, they have ideas about life. Their problem is not really Ole Andreson but the yokels they must deal with; after all, these people have been cluttering up the vaudeville stage longer than living memory. There is no reason to expect them to behave correctly now.

The repetition of one phrase tells us about scripts and other realities:

> "You're a pretty bright boy, aren't you?"
> "Sure," said George.
> "Well, you're not," said the other little man. "Is he, Al?"
> "He's dumb," said Al. He turned back to Nick. "What's your name?"
> "Adams."
> "Another bright boy," Al said. "Ain't he a bright boy, Max?"
> "The town's full of bright boys," Max said. (280)

The vaude tradition pits knowledge against ignorance, so it should not be surprising that at this point the story becomes comic epistemology. As always, the straight man is right: these hicks are dumb enough to believe that the facts of their daily lives correspond to a larger order, that there is a relationship between what they believe and the *actual* context for any belief. This point is large enough to be the story itself, and I will return to it in detail. Here we should sense a kind of intellectual pace: beginning with the usual resentments of comic dialogue we are now moving swiftly to a series of revelations that validate them.

Max catches George looking at him—or perhaps not looking at him—and begins to deliver his philosophical punch lines. They seem at first to be, in the phrase of Edmund Wilson, "pointless"—but pointlessness has a special meaning in the mid-twenties. It illuminates "the way the world is beginning to seem"[27] and goes substantially beyond the subversive way that two-man shows had for a long time "ridiculed middle-class ideals of conduct."[28] This one will ridicule middle-class confidence in a grounded moral world:

> "What are *you* looking it [*sic*]?" Max looked at George.
> "Nothing."
> "The hell you were. You were looking at me."
> "Maybe the boy meant it for a joke, Max," Al said.
> George laughed.
> "*You* don't have to laugh," Max said to him. "*You* don't have to laugh at all, see?"

> "All right," said George.
>
> "So he thinks it's all right." Max turned to Al. "He thinks it's all right. That's a good one."
>
> "Oh, he's a thinker," Al said. They went on eating. (281)

The fundamental breach of decorum is for the rube to laugh; after all, he is the joke, not the audience for the joke. A more serious violation occurs: George is guilty of thinking that anything in the world is "all right" and of wanting "to know what it's all about" (282). He is guilty of being an American after the age of idealism.

There is a splendid remark in Henry F. May's history of thought about the prewar years. Progressive idealists were destined to disappear as intellectual forces, because "two things seemed to bother them in the world of Fitzgerald, Hemingway, and Faulkner: real frivolity and real pessimism."[29] They never understood Hemingway, but he certainly understood them. They represented to him the imposition of morality and politics on criticism and literature. The world he understood was tragic, not idealistic. It can to some extent be understood through its opposites. For example, in "The Killers" we see a world of small-town loyalties and, in some ways, even of heroism. More important, as a brief, sharp, and deeply philosophical passage shows, it is a world understood through certainties:

> "What's the idea?" Nick asked.
>
> "There isn't any idea." (281)

This might qualify as a philosophical problem in any system, and it has to be understood within and opposed to an American tradition of thought. We know that American Idealism in general, and the Public Philosophy in particular, had the deepest concern for grounding action on logical belief. Recent American philosophy had become known for certain kinds of essays on the order of personal and social life, such as, "How to Make Our Ideas Clear" (Charles Sanders Peirce); "Loyalty to

Loyalty, Truth, and Reality" (Josiah Royce); and "The Moral Philosopher and the Moral Life" (William James). There was, one hoped, or should be such an order. In the last of these social statements we see what George and Nick wish to believe: "ordinary men . . . imagine an abstract moral order in which the objective truth resides."[30]

Nick, George, and Sam are ordinary men with an a priori sense of objective truth. They have never examined their own premises because daily life rarely makes one do that. But this story forces them not only to become conscious of their beliefs but to change those beliefs. It forces them to change their idea of logic, which is harder than changing ideas about morality. Much of Hemingway's best work is built around questions that force issues. Dialogue in *A Farewell to Arms* does two kinds of things: it asks questions about the conduct of war, of love, and often of daily life. Characters insistently question each other in the large number of structurally interrogative dialogues. In addition, both implicitly and explicitly the novel conveys that most answers to important issues are not useful. In "The Killers," the questions are of two kinds, tactical and epistemological, both verging on the metaphysical. The tactical questions are about time and the menu, about obeying irrational orders, about going to the movies. There are more than fifty such tactical questions in this story, but they edge into questions of a different order of magnitude, about the nature of things social and universal, about awareness of reality, about the fully human condition. The literature of the first quarter of the century was famous for such questions. Here are some of them as phrased by Josiah Royce: "What do we live for? What is our duty? What is the true ideal of life? What is the true difference between right and wrong? What is the true good which we all need?"[31] Not only are these answerable questions in Royce, *but answering them is itself a moral activity.* The opposite is true in Hemingway, who warns us here and elsewhere that these questions are so difficult—so unreal—that we ought not to think about them. Or, as Sam the cook says in a parable of another sort of wisdom, "You better not have anything to do with it at all" (286). Sam, who is underrated, is intellectually ahead of Nick and George.

Nick and George begin to understand that the two kinds of questions imply each other. When they separately ask, "What's the idea?"

they mean the idea for doing as they are told; but the reader, a party to the dialogue, will understand that the idea refers more to Plato than to Ole Andreson. The idea referred to is the idea of meaning in action and also of meaning in life. That there should be no "idea" for moving behind the counter is an intellectual irritant, but if there is no "idea" for doing or explaining anything or coping with fate, then the problem is much larger. It undercuts the basis for their lives; however, their lives have been both moral and unreflective, which is why Max and Al are so contemptuous of bright boys who are thinkers.

Max and Al, themselves far more intelligent than they appear, know that one kind of question implies the other. To want to know something implies that something is to be known; that a given course of action has a universal consequence; that all parties look at the issue in more or less the same way—although William James, wryly brilliant and in a Hobbesian mood, understood "what the words *good, bad,* and *obligation* severally mean. They mean no absolute natures, independent of personal support. They are objects of feeling and desire which have no foothold or anchorage in Being, apart from the existence of actually living minds."[32] It would be a safe bet that Max and Al know this "idea."

One of the great passages in the story moves with stunning clarity from one form of the same question to its metaphysical shadow:

> "Well, bright boy," Max said, looking into the mirror, "why don't you say something?"
>
> "What's it all about?
>
> "Hey, Al," Max called, "bright boy wants to know what it's all about."
>
> "Why don't you tell him?" Al's voice came from the kitchen.
>
> "What do you think it's all about?'
>
> "I don't know." (282)

By the time this part of the dialogue finishes, Nick realizes that the here and now may not be related to any universal. That particular problem is part of a much larger problem about intelligibility. In 1925, a short time before this story appeared, John Dewey had suggested in an essay on "Nature, Ends and Histories" that the historically naive mind began "with a ready-made list of good things or perfections which it was the business of nature to accomplish."[33] He followed James, who had observed that Americans expect to see in the world the order they so confidently but wrongly impose upon it. The issue was interesting to more than philosophy: Mencken, for example, had recently described our national belief or superstition (he thought it central to our civilization or lack of it) "that right and wrong are immovable things—that they have an actual and unchangeable existence." He suggested, using an interesting metaphor, that to disbelieve in such assumptions was generally interpreted as a kind of "crime against society."[34] Max and Al understand that decision, action, and consequence are relative. Perhaps there is no meaning in life, no morality for causation, no guiding universal. As to the last, reality being purely situational, *there are certain things you never know at the time.*

As Dewey put the matter, it would be deeply confused to think that expectations matched actualities.[35] It would be splendid if the American social order reflected a good and moral universe, but much hard work remained to make the world what one hoped it was. One might fail, at that. Also in 1925, in "Existence, Ideas and Consciousness," Dewey argued that "events which brutely occur and brutely affect us" must be converted into meaning, must have "probable consequences." Otherwise, "philosophy finds itself in a hopeless impasse."[36] Wilson seems to have been purposive and contextual in choosing to state outcomes in terms of their pointlessness. Max and Al may not have been reading either John Dewey or Edmund Wilson, but Hemingway knows about that impasse.

Certain phrases in the story become magnified through repetition and allusion: there is a constant resonance to "what it's all about" and "what's the idea." Readers are intended to recognize that the tactical can become the metaphysical, intended, I think, to move from *what* to *why.* Let us start with a very small and limited *why,* the reason for Max and Al taking bloody murder very much in stride but being offended by ignorance. Is there something visibly characteristic of American life in the provinces that engages them in a way their work does not? They find a laughable disparity between mind and material reality. They suggest that Nick and George may be bright but that they remain boys. Like most straight men, they are adults in a world of children.

Max and Al refer to a subject later mentioned by Walter Lippmann in *A Preface to Morals* (1929) about one persistent aspect of our national character. Americans simply did not want to be aware of the way things actually were. They preferred, in fact, to remain deluded about what "the idea" was for anything. Lippmann thought that Americans generally failed to explain the facts of their lives. We wanted to see an orderly moral world, so we invented one. We ascribed "everything which happens" to "the duty of the universe" toward us; however, the idea that "the universe is full of purposes utterly unknown" seems utterly unknown to Americans. A phenomenon like, let us say, the advent of Max and Al to the town of Summit is a kind of philosophical demonstration that accepted ideas have no authority. Yet, in the terms used by Lippmann, what Max and Al represent "*is in the nature of things.*" Lippmann was to conclude that few Americans could bear to analyze their experience because that would mean the acquisition of a sense of evil.[37] If "The Killers" has a moral—although no great work of art singly does—that would be it.

Evil has many forms. Hemingway's dialogue quickly enters the realm of moral imponderables. Movies, which are entertainment, are in fact explanations. Andreson is going to be killed as part of a professional hence moral obligation. Fate is circumstance:

> "All right," George said, "What are you going to do with us afterward?"
>
> "That'll depend," Max said. "That's one of those things you never know at the time." (284)

Rather small and colorless words carry burdens too large to assess: "do," "afterward," and "depend" mean decisions made as Joseph Conrad imagined them, with one's feet not touching the earth. They do not refer themselves to any "idea," certainly not to justice or meaning, but only to circumstance. The distance between meaning and circumstance is philosophically immense. Max says that he likes George, and he probably does. But Al may yet blow his head off. Why has all this been revealed? "We got to keep amused, haven't we?" (285). The dialogue keeps circling back to the premises of the two-man act, which has more to say here than the hoarded sum of Western moral thought.

My point has consistently been that throughout Hemingway's lifetime, beginning with James and continuing with Dewey, there had been a great, self-conscious and enormously effective attempt to ground the life of democracy precisely *in* those Western moral meanings. Mencken understood that James had defined the meaning of American moral life in a "long and glorious" philosophical reign over the reading audience.[38] Henry Steele Commager (*The American Mind*) gave a new set of bearings when he wrote that, "for a generation no issue was clarified until Dewey had spoken."[39] One silent conclusion of this story is that moral explanations of the kind Dewey and James had so richly provided for America had failed. That is why such explanation is either absent or ineffective and why the premises of idealism and pragmatism are so intensely ridiculed. Outside the story, for its readers, is the enormous moral authority of those who have defined for us the nature of social life, but inside the story they are invisible. The rather large sequence of ideas that George and Nick address—on the meaning of logical action, on universal meaning itself, on the relationship of value to act—have been silently negated. Max and Al replace philosophy. As Edmund Wilson had stated a very short time before, pointlessness is central to the cultural moment.

Both Wilson and Hemingway developed this idea as a conscious part of the not-especially loyal philosophical opposition. They understood that the relationship of reality to idea was that of perception to composition. They knew what they opposed: Dewey "insisted that the world was a world of meaning, not just a world of flatly unintelligible cause and effect connections." It is impossible to understand "The Killers" without reference to that (supposed) fact; however, when we posit order or non-pointlessness in the world, "it is we who are doing all the intellectual work."[40] Max and Al know this, George and Sam and Nick must become painfully educated.

There are few other works of fiction in which meanings are so impacted. A single word implies heroism, as when George, who is asked if Ole Andreson eats here, simply says, "sometimes" and risks his own life. The word "afterward" means the difference between life and death; "They're all right" (285) is nothing less than a special dispensation: it means that George and Nick and Sam will all stay alive because Max knows that they have become realists. George gets the exit line, a rube who has become a straight man: "you better not think about it" (289).

The last line of the story may not be Heidegger, but it is definitely philosophy. It ought to be read against an important passage about American provincial life in Royce, in which we are told that "all of us first learned about what we ought to do, about what our ideal should be, and in general about the moral law" from "our teachers, our parents, our playmates, society, custom, or perhaps some church." But belief does not matter because of its source alone: it remains for us to validate it: "What reason can I give why my duty is my duty?" What makes us human is not what is handed down, but the way the mind works under pressure to "furnish the only valid reason for you to know what is right and good."[41] That is what Nick and George and Sam are asked to deny, and what Max and Al conclude they will deny.

In the single best-known statement of recent American philosophy, *Pragmatism,* William James had referred to a notorious crime involving murder and suicide. He understood plainly that this was both a philosophical and a religious issue. James cited the reaction of a drastically empiricist mind that saw in this crime "one of the elemental stupendous facts of this modern world" that "cannot be glozed over or minimized away by all the treatises on God, and Love, and Being, helplessly existing in their monumental vacuity."[42] Such crimes or existential facts, James writes, constitute a "dilemma" for the American mind, whose sense of the verities of daily life is based on intangibles and unprovables.The governing "idea" of the town of Summit is that of all small towns in the mid-twenties and was stated clearly in the best-known of them all: the assumption that "the world is good, God is good, and His spirit wherein men are to live is love's spirit" becomes embodied in "an elaborate system of beliefs, prohibitions, and group-sanctioned conduct." But, even inside *Middletown* we are always aware that some of the beliefs of this system are impossible to accept literally, "without lying to yourself."[43]

From this dilemma came James's famous statement about American tough-mindedness, a quality that seems to me to describe Hemingway's philosophical stance. The tough-minded were empirical, and in rejecting any systems, they rejected not only explanation but the "idea" of explanation. It may have been only fitting that in 1926 Hemingway too should turn to murder as a philosophical test. James knew that all theories, empiricism among them, and all stances, tough-mindedness among them, were what he called remedies for the world of facts. I believe that Hemingway understood that, but his fiction needed what it found in radical empiricism, which is disguised here as vaudeville philosophy. Or rather, it takes on the appropriate form of vaudeville philosophy.

6

Protestant, Catholic, Jew: *The Sun Also Rises*

Throughout the early and mid-twenties Eliot would react to Unitarian liberalism, Hemingway would satirize the values of provincial Congregationalism, and Fitzgerald would secularize the themes of both Protestant and Catholic idealism. All would in the course of their work deal badly—and in such a way as to compromise the value of that work—with Jews. In Hemingway, the three religions would be connected.

Two conflicts between Catholic and Protestant affected Hemingway in 1925 and 1926. One was the culmination of a public debate on the uses of history and the idea of progress, the other an *affaire* that became charged with literary meanings. Both are important in *The Sun Also Rises*. The "deeply ingrained Catholicism" of Pauline Pfeiffer is said by Michael Reynolds to have "controlled her life."[1] She brought to her relationship with Hemingway a good deal of moral anxiety, causing him to take seriously doctrine, especially of sin, and observance, especially of prayer. He became for a time a convert. As Reynolds sees it, Pauline's ideas were catalytic:

> Pauline was a devout Catholic, and Ernest's profession of faith seemed too convenient. But . . . [not even] doubters thought of Hemingway as a Protestant, and he, himself, never looked back on his Congregational training which he associated with Oak Park hypocrisy, his father's unbearable piety and his mother's church politics of who would rule the choir loft. In

> Italy during his first war, he experienced a country where religion was woven into every facet of the culture. . . . Before Hemingway was involved with Pauline, the ritual, ceremony and mystery of the Catholic Church were a strong attraction for a man who needed all three. As became more obvious later in his life, Hemingway was deeply drawn to all things medieval, which is to say all things ancient and Catholic. Pauline Pfeiffer's presence in his life probably accelerated his profession of faith.[2]

Elsewhere Reynolds notes the specific values of prayer and charity in *The Sun Also Rises* and the large number of incidents in the novel that have to do with religion.[3] H. R. Stoneback describes the period 1917–25 in Hemingway's life as a "bitter rejection of Protestantism and discovery of Catholicism, an awakening to an aesthetic sense centered on ritual and ceremony . . . deepening engagement with the sacramental sense of experience."[4] But, while criticism has cited Catholic ritual and observance, it has tended to ignore ideas and ideology. As in any Hemingway work, the text deals with and argues ideas.

In *The Sun Also Rises* there are formal oppositions between Paris and Pamplona, Jew and Gentile, medieval and modern, and most important, between the values located by Hemingway in Catholicism and those connected with the idea of progress. The last of these pairings had from 1920 to 1926 become part of a public debate. *The Outline of History* by H. G. Wells was at first a success, on the Best Seller list for both 1921 and 1922. For a book no longer read, it has had an impact on the century's mind. *The Outline of History* was a review of the many failures of civilization, but it also was an argument for a new "world order" and "universal law." It was necessarily dismissive of the past, especially of its baggage of religion and tradition. Wells's concern was the shaping of a more rational future; his conclusion describes "The Next Stage of History" and how to get there. From the viewpoint of scientific socialism it was easy to see that "great rearrangements are necessary" because the world as historically constituted was deeply unsatisfactory. These rearrangements had to do with abandoning supposedly primitive forms of human behavior and the institutions guilty of fostering them. For example, "that mere witless killing which is called sport to-day would inevitably give place in a better educated world community to a modification of the primitive instincts that find expression in this way."[5] This might well have been of interest to those adversary presences the "Old Lady" in *Death in the Afternoon* and Robert Cohn in *The Sun Also Rises.* But the *Outline* is full of challenges to a mind like Hemingway's, for it discounts heroism, presumes unearned moral equality, discards the traditional, historical and primitive, and argues tenuously for secular salvation.

Except for the Crusades, it is difficult to find much about the medieval period in Wells's *Outline.* The period was imaginatively important to Eliot, Fitzgerald, Hemingway, and Pound, but it signified to Wells only the recalcitrance of the mind. Like most on the left, he preferred the Renaissance for its utility as a social metaphor. Wells had no feel for medieval art, whereas Hemingway, understanding its relationship to modernism, wrote in 1925, "As for Yeats he and Ezra and Anonymous are my favourite poets." And Hemingway cited at length from what he took to be a definitive form of poetry, the medieval ballad. *The Sun Also Rises* is impacted with medieval images, allusions, echoes—and convictions. In a central way it is a retelling of the story of Eloisa and Abelard, and we are supposed to know what the Song of Roland was about. The enormous aggregate of its medievalism, its sense of the sheer historical mass still imaginatively alive is itself a response to the Wellsian frame of mind. Wells had provided a text like an overgrown *Dial* or *New Republic* to despise.[6]

But Hemingway and others who objected to the limits of "progress" had different texts to consult. Wells had for several years been satirized as efficiently by Hilaire Belloc as Fenimore Cooper and Mary Baker Eddy had been by Mark Twain. By 1926, the year of publication of *A Companion to Mr. Wells's Outline of History,* he had been from the specifically Catholic point of view discredited. A novel about Catholicism and the authority of medieval ideas appearing in that year might well carry a double weight.

In reviewing Wells, Belloc had had both a historical and a doctrinal point of view. The *Outline* suffered because of its ignorance of medieval institutions—but it suffered even more because it viewed the period as a hiccup before modernity. It was fixated on a Victorian prejudice: "there runs through the whole . . . the nineteenth-century idea of 'progress.' It is taken for granted, in all its crudity, all its tautology, all its unproved and untrue postulates, and all its flagrant contrast with reality."[7] The idea of progress was more useful and even more noble than Belloc imagined, but it had become exaggerated and politicized. Reinhold Niebuhr's great synthesis *The Nature and Destiny of Man* observed that it had provoked a demonstrably false certainty on the part of the Enlightenment, "that reason will generate individual virtue" and destroy "superstitions." Victorianism, even when most scientifically disposed, believed with false optimism that "the most tragic conflicts of history" could be resolved into "harmony and progress"[8]

The point of Belloc (and, in a far more sophisticated way, of Hemingway) was that Wells misunderstood both religion and nature. It was idly Utopian to think of change at will, of escaping the fixed boundaries of the self. For example, Belloc insisted that mankind is not "a mere phase in process of passing, but a fixed type with a known nature."[9] That is an idea central to Hemingway, and he took pride in its deployment. In *The Sun Also Rises* the idea underpins character: "Probably I never would have had any trouble if I hadn't run into Brett when they shipped me to England. I suppose she only wanted what she couldn't have. Well, *people were that way.* To hell with people. The Catholic Church had an awfully good way of handling all that."[10] The passage resonates to Belloc, who argued against Wells that "the Catholic Church—lives its whole life by consulting and realizing the common man."[11] And the passage implies much about Robert Cohn and others who think, read, edit, write, and are ignorant of and hostile to preexistent truths.

Belloc was once present in the text of *The Sun Also Rises,* in the beginning section cut from the galleys on the advice of F. Scott Fitzgerald. In a long passage, Braddocks (i.e., Ford Madox Ford) thinks he sees Hilaire Belloc passing by. Fine-tuned to cultural gossip, Braddocks describes him to Jake as a man on the losing side in the wars of religion and literature. For one thing, his reactionary polemics (some violently anti-Semitic) have ensured that "not a review in England will touch him."[12] But Alister Crowley, whom he mistakes for Belloc, turns out to be even more notorious. Why was Belloc invoked by the old beginning?

He was invoked to set the tone of Catholic cultural apologetics and even, I think, to introduce a considered, tactical anti-Semitism. Why Crowley? He was a satanic, sadistic figure involved in cult worship, *which made him Belloc's unacceptable social equivalent.* The cut passage was meant, I think, to suggest not only that Belloc has left tracks in the novel but that the dimly lit mind of Ford—the intellectual mind in general—is clueless. It cannot tell the difference between men or ideas. After the passage was cut, Belloc became the man who wasn't there, but the novel retains his intellectual presence, his values, and his exclusionary beliefs.[13]

The great point of Hemingway's two novels of the twenties is that they argue a particular and highly unsentimental view of human nature. Catholicism is useful in both because it provides an interpretation of human nature consonant with Hemingway's—or productively at odds with him—and superior to that of Wells. It is superior even in the way of ideals: the Abruzzi (in *A Farewell to Arms*) may not be a possible destination, but it is *somewhere.*

Will Herberg's book on American religion—I have borrowed its title for the title of this chapter—remarks that one of the theological problems our country has contributed to world history is the secularization of faith: "From the very beginning the American Way of Life was shaped by the contours of American Protestantism; it may, indeed, best be understood as a kind of secularized Puritanism, a Puritanism without transcendence, without sense of sin or judgment."[14] Hemingway was well aware of this; the evidence in the mid-twenties comes from his short stories, correspondence, and his first novel. When he writes about the values of Catholicism in *The Sun Also Rises,* there is a strong implication that Protestantism fails to understand the issues.[15] There were indeed such failings, if we recall the consistent attempt in the twenties to secularize the gospels, to give boosterism its own theology. As we see in "Soldier's Home" (1924) "business" has been identified with "success," and both business and success, with the values of Christianity.[16] In *The Sun Also Rises,* Hemingway, developing his ideas, tackled a more complex subject, the attractions of a higher Protestant style for the urbane, educated, and unanchored mind.

Hemingway's quarrel with America involved much more than contempt for the limits of Protestantism; it was connected also to Judaism, the last element of the American triad. Especially from 1924 to 1926, if we can judge from references in his correspondence and, of course, in his first novel, he felt impelled to attack Jews. It has become common to diffuse the issue of Hemingway's anti-Semitism, and the superficiality of criticism on this subject can be judged by its willingness to abide by the false idea that the twenties as a whole were anti-Semitic, hence that Hemingway only reflected his moment. Since the recent appearance of two important books on the subject, it has become impossible to remain satisfied with the amorphous idea that, because everyone in the twenties was anti-Semitic, so inevitably was Hemingway. The books I refer to are Bryan Cheyette's *Constructions of "The Jew" in English Literature and Society* and, especially, *T. S. Eliot, Anti-Semitism, and Literary Form* by Anthony Julius.

The book by Julius does two things: it relates the writing of Eliot to the subliterature of the time, and it differentiates between kinds of anti-Semitism. By the early twenties the doctrines of anti-Semitism had evolved considerably. A great range of indictments exists, from the masscult idea that Jews make money dishonestly to that hugely indefinite idea expressed around the turn of the century by J. K. Huysmanns: "I am an anti-Semite, because I am convinced that it is the Jews who have turned France into the sad country, agitated by the lowest passions, the sad country without God, which we now see."[17] Eliot's poetry and prose cover a certain part of the spectrum: Jews tend to be anarchic; they have philistine cultural tastes; their intelligence is tied to no particular set of values; they are gross; their own free-thinking is dangerous for Christians; they are too skeptical to be part of a culture that requires assent; most important, they subscribe to and are wholly identified with the current practices of that liberalism that is in itself an attack on the Christian past. Julius notes the extent to which these beliefs were shared by intellectuals.[18]

Before changes in dress, language, and status allowed for assimilation, Jews had been too different to accept. In Great Britain they had been advised to come out of isolation, civilize themselves, learn English, mix with and adapt to the majority. Having successfully done so, however, they ran into another problem: they were now indistinguishable. Belloc and Chesterton wanted Jews to remain visibly separate. Michael Coren has remarked, in fact, that Chesterton became "terrified that he would encounter a Jew, and not know it."[19] Robert Cohn has assimilated, a special problem for Chesterton and Eliot, for Belloc and Hemingway.[20] Cohn's absorption into America has covered at least two generations. His parents are not recent immigrants, and he is not an eastern Jew from a radically different culture like Poland or Russia, with its own styles and observances. On the contrary, he is a by-now familiar American type, excessively and aggravatingly innocent, self-absorbed, and practicing the national style of fuzzy idealism. Like many secularized Americans, he has visions of improvement and personal change. This makes for a special and highly interesting correlation in Hemingway, because every now and then it is necessary for Cohn to stop being a Jew and become an imitation Protestant. He retains what makes him indefensible but adopts what is unbelievable. That is a large issue in the text of *The Sun Also Rises.*

In this novel, Catholic intellectual authority is leveled against Jewish skeptical presumption in the guise of progressive Protestant style. As one of Hemingway's friends put the matter, he "was a Catholic in those days when the Catholic Church was a church instead of a mass confusion," and "he was a traditional Catholic as we all were at the time."[21] To be a traditionalist at that time implied the acceptance of church authority defining character and action, that is, of dogma governing the *interpretation* of daily life as well as its conduct. One would know instantly about being (as Jake calls himself, under the sting of his failings and sins) "a rotten Catholic." Jake later remarks of Romero that he has his own "system of authority" (185), which allows the events of life to be organized around meaning. Jake too has a place from which to judge and to exert intellectual leverage. He argues with his failings, not his system.

As for Jews and Protestants, Julius's book outlines T. S. Eliot's argument, on display over a period of years and throughout many poems, essays, and observations: (1) a single Jew mentioned in his work stands for all Jews; (2) anti-Semitism is caused by Jews, hence has a defensive and satirical kind of virtue; and (3) Jews represent disintegrative elements in Western culture, and their skepticism endangers social traditions. Hemingway spends a great deal of time in *The Sun Also Rises* developing arguments that resonate to these points.

Scott Donaldson has noted that the novel "is a repository . . . of [Hemingway's own] ethnic and nationalistic prejudices." Individual Canadians are rudely *Canadian;* Germans have their obnoxious *national* character; while to be French is naturally and nationally to grasp after money. The context sets individuals up as groups—although some, Basque and Spanish, benefit from the conjunction of individual with national character.[22] In respect to Cohn, there are certain obvious "signals" to "the American reader in 1926" about his group identity: because he comes from a rich and old New York family he belongs also "to the Jewish establishment, which many thought to be a threat to the American way of life." And his *individual* "dislikable characteristics" are "never" separated from his "Jewishness." In fact, when Michael Reynolds examines the historical context, he concludes flatly that its anti-Semitism is directed not at Cohn as an individual *but at "a rich New York Jew who did not know his place."*[23]

Possibly the best proof is the text itself: Reynolds observes that Bill does not wonder much about the unique attractions of Robert Cohn but, instead, why Brett did not go off "with some of her own people" (102). Mike says that Brett has gone off with men before, "but they weren't ever Jews" (143). Hemingway knew, admired, and imitated Jews from Gertrude Stein to Bernard Berenson. Why he did so, yet wrote anti-Semitic prose and poetry is possibly unknowable. But the text, in its uncompromising use of the plural, is not conjectural: Cohn stands for all Jews.

One of the tactics of Hemingway's narration is to offer corroborating evidence: Jake's supporting cast agrees that Cohn is a dissonant presence both as a Jew and as a man. Bill finds him to be "superior and Jewish" (96), a combination that is expected and irritating; then he asks Jake if he has "some more Jewish friends" (101) who might be just as impossible. Bill is a decent sort and tries a number of times to qualify his disapproval. But Hemingway has made him the voice of opinion: the mere intelligence of Jews, seen by Eliot and other writers as ethically "detached critical intelligence," is without values, hence without value.[24] According to this view, Jews do not have the capacity for belief. (Chesterton's *Manalive* of 1912 suggests that a Jew's reluctance to honor traditions of their host society is a form of "shameless rationality.")[25] In the case of Hemingway, ritual and myth were endangered by Jewish "skepticism." He had both traditions and irrationalities to protect. Like Eliot and like Huysmanns, he is easily led to a position of purely *defensive,* virtuous anti-Semitism. When Robert Cohn is attacked in the novel—he is the cause of attack—it is usually from the point of view of defending manners or even morals.

In regard to Cohn, Jake alternates between hatred and *caritas.* The hatred is ascribed to jealousy, but he spends a good deal of time on Cohn's broken, improved nose (it seems to slow down the beginning of the novel, before anything happens). The preoccupation with Cohn's nose may be meant to suggest another problem entirely, Jake's *agenbite of inwit,* but it is less trivial than it seems, part of what Julius calls the aesthetics of ugliness. That is a (sizeable) category of anti-Semitism offering a way of looking at characters like Eliot's Rachel and Bleistein and Hemingway's Cohn, making them emblematically ugly.[26] The technique, borrowed from cartoons and tracts, is reductive: the sordid, ugly, and comic demand no seriousness, invite little moral retaliation.

Cohn is described as having a "hard, Jewish, stubborn streak" (10), and that too is contextual, derivative: Eliot describes "the hard Semitic bitterness" of another Jewish novelist, Maxwell Bodenheim, as a way of implying that the work is beyond the need to explain, because his identity makes it unnecessary to apply whatever norms of literary criticism might otherwise be applied.[27]

The largest issue is cultural style. Mike says that Cohn has no "manners," a point echoed by Jake who says that "he's behaved very badly" and by Brett who adds that "he had a chance to behave so well" (181). The manners issue shows up in almost every scene: Cohn is uncompanionable, intrusive, a killjoy at the bullfight, an undesired presence in the group. He is phenomenally maladroit with women, playing bridge, talking—doing anything social. He is also a Philistine who does not understand the courtly rules of love. Manners are important as a Jewish issue in the twenties. The problem of manners should be decoded; it is the problem of assimilation. Even where an effort is made, the Jew cannot escape his identity, cannot make the transition to civility and urbanity. He is not "one of us" (a phrase actually used in the novel, but in another context). Léon Poliakov posed a famous question that is, I think, on Hemingway's mind: "are the Jews congenitally unsociable and rude, or are they this way as a result of having been segregated into ghettos?" Certain Jews, self-admittedly, have "little grace and no manners"; they "are not easy to live with." Of others, Walter Lippmann made a famous and personally unhappy observation in 1922: Jewish "behavior in public places" was itself a cause of anti-Semitism. It was incumbent on the Jew, as it is for Cohn in *The Sun Also Rises,* to behave well and not to be "conspicuous" in polite society. Specifically, the assimilated Jew needed to learn "moderation" and "taste." That would lead to "sympathetic understanding" by others.[28]

Cohen has failed in "moderation" and "taste." In an evocative line, Brett says, "I hate him, too, . . . I hate his damned suffering" (182). What she says is extraordinary (the illiberal relationship of hatred to suffering) unless the context is figured in. She has transparently been given the language of a social code: Undeserved self-pity, as Kipling would write a few years later, is a rightly despised characteristic of the Jewish liberal mind.[29] The point is made more than once: Cohn enjoys or practices suffering because that is a form of passive aggressiveness. He has been the transgressor.

These are some of the Jewish issues.[30] There are then the Protestant issues, or ways in which Cohn merges his own identity with that to which he aspires. Texts are guides: in *The Sun Also Rises* Harvey Stone reads Mencken, is even prescient about his reputation; Jake reads Turgenieff whose style and values imply his own; but Robert Cohn, an indiscriminate man and reader, has found a different kind of guide to life:

> He had been reading W. H. Hudson. That sounds like an innocent occupation, but Cohn had read and reread "The Purple Land." "The Purple Land" is a very sinister book if read too late in life. It recounts splendid imaginary amorous adventures

> of a perfect English gentleman in an intensely romantic land, the scenery of which is very well described. For a man to take it at thirty-four as a guide-book to what life holds is about as safe as it would be for a man of the same age to enter Wall Street direct from a French convent, equipped with a complete set of the more practical Alger books. Cohn, I believe, took every word of "The Purple Land" as literally as though it been an R. G. Dun report. (9)

Books matter a great deal as referents in Hemingway; and Alger, Hudson, and R. G. Dun seem to be the texts that structure Cohn's mind. Their themes of success, romance and rebirth, and money combine Jewish and Protestant stereotypes. The Alger books are especially useful to Hemingway because they retell a story essential to understand Cohn. We want to recall that Alger heroes, quintessentially American-Protestant, know how to box in defense of the virtues. It is a set piece in the novels: in *Sink or Swim* our hero faces a bully whose "sentiment of honor was not very keen." "Flinging out blows at random" he is in a few moments, however, quite "prostrate."[31] In *Strong and Steady; Or, Paddle Your Own Canoe* the villain—particularly loathsome this time—also delivers "his blows at random" but also soon lies "prostrate" on the ground. This particular fight is accompanied by a long and immensely useful apologetic in which the hero argues that knocking a man down is the only conceivable way to answer aspersions about his condition.[32] In fact, the defining characteristic of gentility is the ability to defend one's claim to it. This comes a generation before Teddy Roosevelt. It is bourgeois chivalry, and the Alger books with their combination of honor and success, may well be, as Hemingway suggests, on Robert Cohn's mind. They are myths of remaking the self. And they are a strand in the larger theme of Religion and the Rise of Capitalism—which became a famous idea (and text) of 1926.

Nevertheless, it is the Hudson book that gets top billing, a parody of New World rebirth and radical innocence. *The Purple Land* keeps on echoing in Hemingway's own text as Cohn insists on applying it to life. Most of the second chapter is about its themes: Cohn is desperate for emotional rebirth and actually wants Jake to go with him to a (Promised) Purple Land. The issues are serious, although the ideas are comical. When Cohn says that "I can't stand it to think my life is going so fast and I'm not really living it" (10), he is at least on the verge of a spiritual insight. But Jews evidently do not have the Augustinian equipment to understand life. Jake does:

> "Listen, Robert, going to another country doesn't make any difference. I've tried all that. You can't get away from yourself by moving from one place to another. There's nothing to that."
>
> "But you've never been to South America."
>
> "South America hell! If you went there the way you feel now it would be exactly the same." (11)

Cohn hates Paris but loves a place he has never been.[33] This kind of potentialism had been described in 1920 by George Santayana, long a critic of Protestant optimism from a Catholic viewpoint, who discriminated between ridiculous idealism that was located merely "in the region of hope" and idealism more solidly established in the "region of perception and memory." The man who argues from hope only "idealises *a priori,* is incapable of true prophecy; when he dreams he raves, and the more he criticises the less he helps."[34]

W. H. Hudson's ideas were certainly located in the region of hope. Both *The Purple Land* and *Green Mansions* seem to be on Robert Cohn's mind and both exemplify the final attenuation of Victorian idealism. The former appeared the same year as *King Solomon's Mines* and only two years before Rider Haggard's highly accomplished *Allan Quatermain.* It suffers greatly by comparison, although it deals with some of the same ideas about renewal and the romantic quest. Hemingway was, I think, trying to direct us to a central fallacy established in Hudson's opening pages: "Something came to rouse me from the state I was in, during which I had been like one that has outlived his activities, and is no longer capable of a new emotion, but feeds wholly on the past. . . . I was like one who, opening his eyes from a troubled doze, unexpectedly sees the morning star in its unearthly lustre . . . the star of day and everlasting hope and of passion and strife and toil and rest and happiness."[35] In the midst of this our mortal life I became lost among unfriendly nouns. Hudson represents late Victorian medievalizing, which had diminished itself into romance, become sentimental and secular.

Hemingway's text states that Robert Cohn "took every word" (9) of *The Purple Land* "literally," an allusion to more than romantic escapism. That Dantean yearning for a new life describes Cohn's uncritical mind. He may know the story literally, but I think that for Jake Barnes he exemplifies it figuratively. Cohn too wants to be transformed, but the issue resolves itself into one of social identity: he wants not only to escape Paris and the civilized condition but to escape himself as he is seen by others. Cohn is a rootless Jew (it was a favorite conception of Eliot's) who imitates exhausted Protestantism, which imitates a spiritual quest understandable only in terms of Catholic authenticity. Cohn's relationship to place is equivocal: his family comes from Europe, lives in New York, sends him to Paris where he dreams of South America. As in Eliot, the spatial suggests the spiritual. Carlos Baker's great study of Hemingway places this novel under the rubric of "The Wastelanders," and clearly the comparison needs to be taken in detail.

Cohn has self-doubt to which Jake clearly responds, but the main thing about Cohen is his aspiration to the wrong model for change. In 1929, Reinhold Niebuhr reviewed the thought of the past decade about regenerating the civilized self. Himself critical of the Protestant moment, he was profoundly unsympathetic to the idea, drawing upon Schweitzer and Whitehead to refute theories that had endowed moderns with a priori idealism. (This idealism was to become a problem for Jews in the next decade, but in the twenties, it was largely a Protestant issue). According to Niebuhr, "Albert Schweitzer interprets the whole moral bankruptcy of Western civilization as a pessimistic reaction to the extravagant optimism of its traditional religions and philosophies." Any regeneration will definitely *not* come from "the sentimentality of an unqualified optimism."[36] There is an important passage which follows, about the gain and loss of ideas from medieval Christianity. It deals with that current Protestant optimism that in Robert Cohn so singularly qualifies his "Jewish" skepticism: "There was something lacking in Spencerian optimism which is very vital to religion, a sense of the tragic in life and an awareness of the frustration which moral purpose and creative will must meet in nature and in man. The sentimentality of modern religion is of course older than the optimism which it derived from Spencer. Part of it derived from Rousseau and the romanticism of the eighteenth century. . . . modern churches are involved in an optimistic overestimate of the virtue of both man and nature at the very time when science tempts men to despair."[37] Cohn does not have a "sense of the tragic in life," whereas Jake has in abundance "an awareness of the frustration which moral purpose and creative will must meet in nature and man." Cohn dreams of personal change, whereas Jake understands the unyielding way we are through dogma and doctrine. The myth of personal change is unreal enough, but it is compounded by the issue of Jewish identity disguised by the assimilated style.

Some of Robert Cohn's problems are native, but possibly the most serious ones arise from his assimilation of and to the wrong models. He exemplifies false chivalry. When Cohn's attraction to Brett is described, we see "the childish, drunken heroics of it. It was his affair with a lady of title." And there is Cohn's romantic-medieval readiness "to do battle for his lady love" (178). The last word on this subject has, I think, been written by Mark Girouard whose book *The Return of Camelot* exhaustively considers the ways in which late Victorianism—the source of Cohn's imagination—imitated medievalism.[38] There was a trove to draw on of sappy posters of knights (literally) in shining armor designed to promote enlistment from the Boer War to the Great War; of doggerel and boys' stories like those that Orwell read defending virtue and Empire; and of discourse as common as that of Meyer Wolfshiem (!) praising gentlemen "of fine breeding." Religious themes became cultural themes. Hemingway knows this and has concentrated thematically on manner, courtly love, and the derisory fate of the *vita nuova.*

The important point for late Victorian medievalizing (at least in theory) was social mobility: "anyone who lived up to the standards of a gentleman automatically became one."[39] There were infallible indicators: obeying rules and social standards; caring for self and others; and, pace Robert Cohn, chivalry to women. Hemingway is nevertheless attentive to distinctions. Whereas a true British gentleman, for example, was to be known by his excellence at the "manly sports" and at social games, there is Cohn's unthinkable boasting about making a living at cards. Jewish identity and Protestant aspiration make a bad mix: he is a fake gentleman, not, after all, that "perfect English gentleman" of W. H. Hudson's and his own imaginings.

Girouard states that upward social mobility had become an economic fact that required social authentication. In other words, before middle-class Jews could become Protestants, aspiring Protestants had to become gentlemen. The chivalric model became highly useful in establishing the right to social style, hence to class, and a way of asserting belief and substance through manner. Two kinds of assimilation were involved. The first was closer to Hemingway than we may think. It is described, memorably, in a letter by his mother:

> Stop trading on your handsome face, to fool little gullible girls, and neglecting your duties to God and your Saviour Jesus Christ. . . .
>
> This world, which is your world, is crying out for men, real men, with brawn and muscle, moral as well as physical—men whose mothers can look up to them, instead of hanging their heads in shame at having borne them. Purity of speech and life, have been taught you from earliest childhood. You are born of a race of gentlemen. . . . clean mouthed, chivalrous to all women, grateful and generous . . . See to it that you do not disgrace their memories.[40]

Cohn's imitation of genteel chivalry has a good deal to do with Grace Hall Hemingway's understanding of high culture. Hemingway himself understands exactly which models of identity are being proposed and what someone might do to fit into a "world" of "race." Cohn becomes or tries to become what Hemingway refused to become.

The combination of chivalry, romance, and *machismo* is an upscale version of muscular Christianity. We might call it Protestantism gone to Princeton. Cohn adds to it other culturally acquired ideals, including those of progressive American intellectuals toward the bullfight. Here, for example, is Robert Benchley at the *corrida* in an earlier moral incarnation, at a time when he was still much under the influence of progressive cultural pieties: "I left wishing I could touch a button that would topple the whole place over on top of the crowd and bury them all."[41]

But Hemingway insists on remaking the point that the relationship of Protestant style and Jewish identity does not work: when things go bad for Cohn acting the gent, "his face had the sallow, yellow look it got when he was insulted, but somehow he seemed to be enjoying it" (178). This is said coldly and in retrospect. It is a pretty bad moment, even for readers of the twenties. We are back to Eliot and Belloc and Chesterton but also past them, in the gutter anti-Semitism which ascribes pleasure to suffering. There are lines about Jews in the subliterature of anti-Semitism cited by Julius and by Hannah Arendt in *The Origins of Totalitarianism* that are by no means as bad. The joke for Jake and Bill, and also for Brett, is the Jewish sheep in wolf's clothing, the disguise of honor for someone incapable of understanding it.

All this is to say nothing of paganism, which may be the fourth religion in the book[42]; however, it is, I think, subsumed here as in historical fact by the absorptive powers of Catholicism.

Although Hemingway has a strategic purpose, which is to express character through belief and cultural style, he is unable to fulfill that tactically. One of the larger problems is that Robert Cohn is not given enough of an argument to state. Most of what we know about him comes at second hand, from others in the story. They decide for us what his character means. After the first few chapters, Cohn becomes as much object as subject; and there is not much to correlate with what he is said so trivially to express. Hemingway gets lost in purposes, devoting an enormous amount of description to Cohn's relationship with women, which would seem to argue some kind of sexual motivation (and attraction). Nothing is made of this, although something else is brilliantly intimated: as a novelist, writer, and universal victim of women, Cohn brings out what has elsewhere been called the "impotently genteel and feminized" aspect of American character and letters.[43] He seems to represent the kind of superficial cultural literacy that Hemingway despised, to be a test case for it—a literary Macomber; however, Hemingway himself made Cohn a representative figure rather than a fully motivated personality. Ideas have been attributed to Cohn, and in some respects he remains an idea—and an interesting idea at that, one that was very much on the mind of Grace Hall Hemingway.

Cohn unaccountably hates Paris and "would rather have been in America" (5), another idea he gets from books. Is he like Dorothy Parker or Robert Benchley, simply at a loss in Europe, spiritually disarmed? Parker, obtrusively both Jewish and Protestant, later reacted to Spain in life as Cohn does in the novel.[44] But the issue seems more directly connected to the cultural politics of the early twenties. A model exists for this particular situation: Santayana had written with some contempt that any intellectually serious American should leave home and go "to Oxford or Florence or Montmartre to save his soul" (or perhaps, more interestingly, "not to save it"); however, there are, he says, those who hate Paris, and he is particularly critical of them. The ugly American wants to return home; desperate for the comforts of what Santayana identifies as the wreckage of Protestant idealism. Americans who have been exposed to European civilization, with its harder moral edges, want necessarily to return to that infinitely jejune "belief in progress" that is the sole surviving idea of their national religion.[45] History itself makes them morally uncomfortable. The central argument between liberal Protestantism and Spanish Catholicism was perceived some years later by Salvador de Madariaga, who wrote that Hemingway refused to be "the Protestant ever ready to frown at Catholic superstition, the progressive commiserating on backward Spain,"[46] in other words, a Benchley, a Parker, or a Robert Cohn—or another collateral descendant of H. G. Wells.

7

Order and Will in *A Farewell to Arms*

The first half-dozen chapters of *A Farewell to Arms* pose certain questions. Frederic Henry has not been to a battle like the Somme, and Caporetto has not yet occurred. Yet he is suffering from something, although it is not battle fatigue. Possibly it is from the other war that Rinaldi describes as "nothing but frostbites, chilblains, jaundice, gonorrhea, self-inflicted wounds, pneumonia and hard and soft chancres" (12).[1] Such things eventually force even the relentlessly scientific Rinaldi to break down, whereas Henry seems able to live through them unmoved. Self-control is a stoic virtue—but why is Henry silent, without will, without much feeling or any fellow-feeling? Does his emotional and moral passivity—really paralysis—derive from the shock of war at all, or is it a condition drawn from the period between the time of the novel, 1917, and its writing more than a decade later? Finally, does the text recall only the Great War, or does it superimpose other things on that experience?

It is not about shell-shock or, as Michael Reynolds has pointed out, about battlefield experience at the sites described. The text depicts Frederic Henry's withdrawn consciousness, which devolves into silence and even entropy; and it seems aware of what Freud had at the beginning of the war identified as the form that "disillusionment" was bound to take, namely, rejection of conventional personal values.[2] *A Farewell to Arms* is also a farewell to previous beliefs, social and political. Its language of existential and moral insentience will often make points argued by philosophy. Frederic Henry has for a long time felt very little about anything, including the following subject:

> "Have you ever loved any one?"
> "No," I said. (19).

It is always possible that this statement is a sexual tactic, not true. Ironies aside, Frederic Henry is in some ways even more "scientific" than Rinaldi, a perceiving machine seeing everything while feeling nothing.

The novel deploys known ideas about subjectivity; about emotional and intellectual inertia; about failure at what is now in a febrile way called "communication." These concepts had been debated for a generation. They took different form and used different terminologies, but they were about the work of the will and the capacity to relate the self to people and ideas. It will be best to start just before the publication of *A Farewell to Arms,* with the prescient Edmund Wilson thinking over in a letter to Maxwell Perkins the way that literature was losing its will to be material, moral, and public. The letter is about the book that was to become *Axel's Castle.* Wilson describes a strange new climate of "resignationism" or the "discouragement of the will." The phrases are loaded with references to the disintegrating heritage of American idealism and Idealism. Here is Wilson's account of the literary situation as the year 1929 approached:

> We have now arrived . . . just about where they were with Romanticism a hundred years ago. . . . The generation since the war go in for introspection: they study themselves, not other people: all the treasures, from their point of view, are to be found in solitary contemplation, not in any effort to grapple with the problems of the general life. . . . [Subjectivity] has led to a kind of resignationism in regard to the world at large, in fact, to that discouragement of the will of which Yeats is always talking. . . . The heroes of these writers never act on their fellows, their thoughts never pass into action.

> This is partly, I believe, the effect of the war, either acting directly on the writers themselves or acting on the literary public. . . . This raises general political and social questions [about the paralysis of] the will. . . . .[3]

Particular phrases and ideas allow us to place this passage: Although resolutely a modern, Wilson retained an older mental vocabulary of subjectivity, solitariness, and especially of "the will"—that phrase made famous by the Public Philosophy of James and Lippmann. What he refers to bears on *A Farewell to Arms* because, in that book, Hemingway silently introduces issues more extensive than the experience of war.

Those issues raised by Wilson had been long argued, but in a somewhat different language. In the most influential psychology text before Freud, James had stated his own anxieties about the problem of modern character and "the closed individuality of each personal consciousness." He centered these problems, as Wilson does in the cited passage, on the will. He believed that one of the great problems of American life was our weakened relationship to things and beings outside ourselves. Modernity encouraged isolation and emotional indifference. For James, the ideal was to be "like trees in the forest," independently alive—yet with out roots commingled "in the darkness underground."[4] It is a splendid psychic passage, but James knew the difficulty of our being "continuous" with one another. It may seem like lèse-majesté to intrude the name of Fitzgerald's Josephine Perry among those of Edmund Wilson, William James, and Hemingway, but she does seem in "Emotional Bankruptcy" (1931) to belong there. If the following from that aptly named story were listed along with lines from *A Farewell to Arms,* few readers might detect its origin: "I don't feel anything at all."[5] At the turn of century William James and others worried about the diminishing modern capacity to feel anything; by the end of the twenties, Wilson, Hemingway, and Fitzgerald were to depict the issue in their fiction. When Frederic Henry says, in the brief passage I have cited, that he has never loved anyone, irony is not intended; nor is there an indirect allusion to the emotionally crippling effect of the war. Both question and answer reverberate in Hemingway's writing of the twenties. In two stories of

1924 they are premonitory: "The End of Something" has Nick tell Marjorie "No" to the question of love; and "Soldier's Home" frames the same "No" to the same question. In the latter, Krebs, remarks, "I don't love anybody," cutting off even the possibility.[6]

There are different explanations, listed in ascending order of persuasive power: Kenneth Lynn states that Krebs enacts Hemingway's own escape from the suffocation of motherly love; Michael Reynolds states that Krebs has been affected by the overpowering fear of trench warfare; and James R. Mellow states that sexual experience in Europe after the war has made it impossible for Krebs ever again to be sentimental.[7] The prolonged unconsciousness that Krebs learns to desire, punctuated by occasional sexual pleasure, does not require relationship. It is unlikely that this realization has been caused by war, although war may have been a catalyst. Krebs simply wants a life that is not—Hemingway's phrasing is instructive—"complicated" by otherness. Clear-sighted, without religion, he is also without will, another useless imperative from the past.

The opening chapters of *A Farewell to Arms* describe life behind the lines in 1917 but are concerned with the way that a *contemporary* American mind reacts to that life. As in "The Short Happy Life of Francis Macomber" Hemingway uses an exotic scene to open up a familiar subject. He had many sources of contemporary ideas about denatured Americans to draw upon, and one point of the novel is its reactivity. What, for example, are we intended to think of some pointed references in the text, like the following: "That night at the mess I sat next to the priest and he was disappointed and suddenly hurt that I had not gone to the Abruzzi. . . . I myself felt as badly as he did and could not understand why I had not gone. It was what I had wanted to do." Or, in continuation, "I explained, winefully, how we did not do the things we wanted to do; we never did such things" (13). In these passages, the language of Jamesian psychology has been borrowed and calls attention to itself. The subject is meant to be reflexively familiar: Frederic Henry understands not only the distance between ideal behavior and real behavior but also the distance between will and act described by Wilson. That distance had been measured for over a generation.

In "The Obstructed Will," a central part of his major work on psychology, William James had combined mind, morals, and literature. It was to become a familiar combination in his essays. He states here, "in such characters as Rousseau and Restif it would seem as if the lower motives had all the impulsive efficacy in their hands. Like trains with the right of way, they retain exclusive possession of the track. The more ideal motives exist alongside of them in profusion, but they never get switched on." In a striking premonition of both Conrad and Eliot he added, such "inert" characters have "the consciousness of inward hollowness." He drew a sharp distinction between the pursuit of pleasure and the avoidance of pain: inert character does not seek pleasure but unconsciousness. Character is its own adversary. In one of his best-known passages James had stated, "I have put the thing in this ultra-simple way because I want more than anything else to emphasize the fact that volition is primarily a relation, not between our Self and extra-mental matter (as many philosophers still maintain), but between our Self and our own states of mind."[8] Was that any longer useful?

This Jamesian belief remained influential; in the case of Fitzgerald, it was intellectually dominant, and in that of Edmund Wilson, powerfully reminiscent. Like James, Wilson thought of "normal existence" as the realm of "non-thinking and non-feeling, the laziness of bodily processes inertly fulfilling their functions, of the consciousness inertly drifting."[9] The issue of will may account for Hemingway saying ironically as late as 1941 that *A Farewell to Arms* was "an immoral book." It was not immoral for the reasons usually adduced—drinking, whoring, blasphemy, lying and idleness. Nor was it immoral because of language and depiction.[10] It was immoral because it depicted a modernist sensibility indifferent to abstractions about human nature, otherwise sensed as values.

Argument on the moral sensibility of Americans had begun well before the war. In 1904, William James had warned that "I seem to read the signs of a great unsettlement," concluding that our national lives might easily be confused with an aggregate of solipsisms. He suggested that the new radical empiricism, with its intense rejection of any ideals or universals, might speak for a new generation. Life might become understood solely through "a philosophy of pure experience."[11] That would necessarily make "an immoral book," much harder for Americans to take than contempt for public phrases in common use like "sacred, glorious, and sacrifice and the expression in vain."

The "immorality" goes deeper. James posited a kind of theater of the self in which a highly dramatic encounter occurs between desires and conscience. "The cooling advice which we get from others" leads actually to internal debate between sexual passion and "reasonable ideas." Consciousness is engaged, and the passions have to come to terms with their interlocutors. Reason in James even has some (deeply Victorian) lines to deliver: "Halt! give up! leave off!"[12] Sexual and other passions become abashed or at least they become consciously acknowledged. Not in Hemingway, however, who sets up the issue in the opening chapters of *A Farewell to Arms,* draws attention to the psychological and moral basis of the dialogue—even combines James with Freud by naming a "priest" within that dialogue—and neutralizes it. Frederic Henry is reminded of the good life in a good place, but instead, "I had gone to no such place but to the smoke of cafés and nights when the room whirled and you needed to look at the wall to make it stop, nights in bed, drunk, when you knew that that was all there was" (13). This is not, however, entirely a moral issue, because we know by 1929 that the unreasonable matters at least as much as the reasonable, and what is reasonable in any case no longer has the power of conviction. The dialogue of will is there, carefully restated, but now has a different and more naturalistic conclusion.

Long before anything has happened we begin to understand the various aspects of the problem. The following is not simply descriptive but in some ways diagnostic: "I came back the next afternoon from our first mountain post and stopped the car at the *smistimento* where the wounded and sick were sorted by their papers and the papers marked for the different hospitals. I had been driving and I sat in the car and the driver took the papers in. It was a hot day and the sky was very bright and blue and the road was white and dusty. I sat in the high seat of the Fiat and thought about nothing" (33). These lines coexist with others depicting intense subjectivity, distancing from perceived objects, passivity, the refusal to impose values (derived from now-ineffective idealism) upon experience. They are about the solitary condition.[13] Of this, both James and Dewey had much to say. In "The Moral Philosopher and the Moral Life" James in fact discussed the condition he called "moral solitude." As he put the issue, if a thinker is not consciously responsive to impulse then he may as well think he is a god, detached from human connections. His only problem will be "the consistency of his own several ideals with one another." James adds that some of these will conflict with the rest, and may even "return to haunt him"; and yet, "beyond the facts of his own subjectivity there is nothing moral in the world."[14] Frederic Henry plays out this dilemma. His own experience has been projected against the explanations provided by prewar orthodoxy.

Here is a summary of the later work of Dewey on the failure of the solitary mind: "experience is meaningful: communication pervades experience, events become objects with meaning, experience is 'funded.' The relations and consequences of an object . . . can become the very meaning (both referential and immanent) of the thing itself."[15] That is to say, whether among Romantics or Idealists or, as Dewey hoped, among an educated citizenry, experiences can be experienced only when conveyed, or when shared. We want to remember that phrase "objects with meaning." Very little experience has been funded in this novel, and few objects have any meaning at all.

The first two chapters of *A Farewell to Arms* are precise when they depict the passage of time over a landscape perceived. It might be difficult even for photography to duplicate their restrained factuality: "I saw a cloud coming over the mountain. It came very fast and the sun went a dull yellow and then everything was gray and the sky was covered and the cloud came on down the mountain and suddenly we were in it and it was snow. The snow slanted across the wind, the bare ground was covered, the stumps of trees projected, there was snow on the guns and there were paths in the snow going back to the latrines behind trenches" (6). But there are no "relations and consequences." Hemingway has described absolute subjectivity rendered through absolute objectivity. Nothing perceived has an effect on the mind perceiving it. Perception is enhanced (it is very nearly perfect), but feeling is so delimited as to enforce the idea or sensation that there are no connections between what is seen and the eye seeing it. After many such passages, the refusal to value essences may be, after all, too radically empirical. Nothing here means anything, and that itself is a statement of considerable purpose. Put another way, what we see is disconnected from what we are. Hemingway is not solitary because he is alone; he is solitary in a way no Romantic could possibly comprehend, because his being recognizes no tangencies with being outside itself.

When the writings of William James on subjectivity without will rebound throughout the lifetime of Hemingway; when in 1926 John Dewey wonders aloud in one of his most famous essays about the declining power of idealization for established institutions, *stating that the words "sacred" and "holy" can't really be used about national purposes anymore;* when in 1928 Edmund Wilson writes about our literature of "exhaustion;" when in 1930 he despairs about its ability to deal with "large political, social, moral, and aesthetic questions"; and when in 1929–30 Freud states the limits of the pleasure principle—"against the suffering which may come upon one from human relationships the readiest safeguard is voluntary isolation, keeping oneself aloof from other people . . . turning away"[16]—then certain conclusions begin to impose themselves. *A Farewell to Arms* has many echoes. It illustrates at least two problems. The first was the winding-down of American character, its increasing passivity, alienation, and self-concern. The second and related problem was the failure of norms in the face of reality.

In 1931, in the book that became *Axel's Castle,* Wilson began his study of modernism by applying some of the ideas of A. N. Whitehead to the subject of landscape:

> There is no real dualism, says Whitehead, between external lakes and hills, on the one hand, and personal feelings, on the other: human feelings and inanimate objects are interdependent and developing together in some fashion of which our traditional notions of laws of cause and effect, of dualities of mind and matter or of body and soul, can give us no true idea. The Romantic poet, then, with his turbid or opalescent language, his sympathies and passions which cause him to seem to merge with his surroundings, is the prophet of a new insight into nature: he is describing things as they really are; and a revolution in the imagery of poetry is in reality a revolution in metaphysics. Whitehead drops the story at this point; but he has provided the key to what follows.[17]

Against this contemporary view should be set the scientific and anti-Romantic ideas of the great modernists, who believed that the primary purpose of late nineteenth-century art was *not* "to communicate the emotional excitement of the artist . . . [so that] the recording of nature is secondary."[18] The landscape of *A Farewell to Arms* is decidedly objective but in its own way full of meaning and with an entirely different set of emotions and impressionistic ideas. It might be said that emotions are so delimited as to force a different sense of their own definition:

> The trunks of the trees too were dusty and the leaves fell early that year and we saw the troops marching along the road and the dust rising and leaves, stirred by the breeze, falling and the soldiers marching and afterward the road bare and white except for the leaves. (3)
>
> There was fighting for that mountain too, but it was not successful, and in the fall when the rains came the leaves all fell from the chestnut trees and the branches were bare and the trunks black with rain. The vineyards were thin and bare-branched too and all the country wet and brown and dead with the autumn. (4)

These are intellectually large passages, and they begin with the beginning:

> . . . why ask of my generation?
> As is the generation of leaves, so is that of humanity.
> The wind scatters the leaves on the ground, but the live
> timber
> burgeons with leaves again in the season of spring
> returning.
> So one generation of men will grow while another
> dies.[19]

Hemingway's practice was often to reroute passages from the past, and to compare himself, not invidiously, with Tolstoy or Turgeniev. He is very much up to comparing his writing with Homer. But a dialogue with certain dynamics has been turned into a meditation, and the cycle of life has been negated. As Wilson implies, landscape and humanity are intertwined. But (and this sounds as if Wilson had Hemingway's language in mind) things have been described "as they really are"; and if that is the way they really are at the moment of their description, the old connections have failed to hold. I am not speaking of any duty that Hemingway has to be faithful to Homer, only about his refusal to engage in Wilson's enterprise of making sense out of communicated perception. Life and death move into each other so silently as the language develops; and so little value is wasted on this, that the studied neutrality of description becomes an almost impossible neutrality of feeling and conception. Throughout this novel Hemingway wants to tell us about humanity in landscape and also about the deadened feelings that his narrator has about his perceptions. This goes beyond the studied objectivity of modernism. We are meant to understand that Henry is himself alone. This, however, is itself a problem. Both James and Dewey, unavoidable figures in the history of American thought, had endowed the present with doubts about anyone being himself alone.

Their thought was philosophically but not existentially persuasive. The isolation of Frederic Henry is, I think, the central problem of *A Farewell to Arms*. Edmund Wilson got his ideas about the solitary imagination from Whitehead, whose *Science and the Modern World* observes that it is clearly a by-product of modernity—a form of moral "relativity." Whitehead adds, "Of course, with the exception of those who are content with themselves as forming the entire universe, solitary amid nothing, everyone wants to struggle back to some sort of objectivist position. I do not understand how a common world of thought can be established in the absence of a common world of sense."[20] Whitehead's conclusion depends on a sense of things now lost.

Before Frederic Henry's psychology can be debated, his solipsistic, honest philosophy needs outlining. It certainly is true that Henry invites psychological explanation. One notes that our language of psychological explanation has changed drastically. Kenneth Lynn's 1987 biography of Hemingway makes its point in terms of current terminology: "the portrait of Frederic Henry is a study in affective disorder, and retreat and desertion are functions of a larger disengagement from life."[21] A variety of diagnostic choices have been posed by Hemingway scholarship between "Bergsonian intuitionism, which deprecates mind as an unfortunate limiting agent; pragmatism, which has its locus in action and the results of action; the once popular crude Watsonian behaviorism and its more refined replacement, positivism; phenomenology, with its abdication of all interpretation and evaluation; and existentialism, with its concern for certain emotional states."[22] Nevertheless, one of the most useful combinations of ideas for psychology in fiction had been long provided. In terms of Jamesian psychology and Lippmann's sociology, Frederic Henry is perfectly capable of functioning; he is the last of the great figures of the decade of the twenties whose lives exemplify "drift" rather than navigation.

The term "drift," a trademark of William James, was, as I have noted, redeveloped by Lippmann and Dewey, and it is referenced by Fitzgerald in *The Great Gatsby.* The *locus classicus* is in James, who wrote that without our own adversarial consciousness all thought "would slip away." As he put it, our "spontaneous drift is towards repose," and we have a natural tendency to evade responsibility, consciousness, and action, a tendency which must be fought by the exertion of will. Frederic Henry is particularly opposed to what James had called "simultaneous possibilities," the comparison, selection, and even suppression of which identified a mature mind.[23]

John Dewey updated (and moralized) the point in his "Search for the Great Community" of 1926, stating that "There is a social pathology which. . . . manifests itself in a thousand ways . . . in impotent drifting, in uneasy snatching at distractions . . . in riotous glorification of things 'as they are,' . . . ways which depress and dissipate thought." It led, he thought, to an ungoverned life composed principally of "rationalizations."[24] It cuts close to the bone of contemporary fiction. Hemingway found the idea of drift useful—and also, as Dewey intended, psychologically compelling. He certainly understands the meaning of "will," but he understands also the *necessity* of its failure in a real world.

Jamesian psychology states, "the cognitive faculty, where it appears to exist at all, appears but as one element in an organic mental whole, and as a minister to higher mental powers—the powers of will."[25] James and Dewey may seem morally over-determined (Kenneth Lynn may be quite right in his more clinical diagnosis), but we need them to get at Hemingway. The problem of Frederic Henry is will, which he has himself already described: "We did not do the things we wanted to do; we never did such things" (13). Cognitively, he has no superior in fiction; however, he has no faith in will ("I did not care what I was getting into" [30]), which is the point for ethics in the first quarter of our century. He is in that condition of "moral solitude" foretold by James and remarked by Edmund Wilson. In a passage full of subtle refractions of meaning, it is also directly implied by Rinaldi. In this case, Rinaldi does not act as a scientist:

> He stood up and sat down on the bed. "The knee itself is a good job." He was through with the knee. "Tell me all about everything."
>
> "There's nothing to tell," I said. "I've led a quiet life."
>
> "You act like a married man," he said. "What's the matter with you?"
>
> "Nothing," I said, "What's the matter with you?"
>
> "This war is killing me," Rinaldi said, "I am very depressed by it." He folded his hands over his knee.
>
> "Oh," I said.
>
> "What's the matter? Can't I even have human impulses?" (167)

When Rinaldi states that last phrase he implicitly leaves Henry out of it. And when Henry talks about "nothing" and the meaning of "nothing" he may well mean it. The difference between what Henry has experienced and what he has communicated illuminates Dewey's test case about experience becoming real only when objectified through language. But, Hemingway implies, who cares if Dewey is right? "A quiet life" of absolute subjectivity may be the only possible life and silence the only possible attitude.

Can a case be made *for* Frederic Henry? Is there something in his self-examining honesty that is intellectually valuable if not redemptive? On another part of the Italian front, Ludwig Wittgenstein wrote of the difference between his state of self-consciousness in 1916 and 1918: "I am now *slightly* more decent. By this, I only mean that I am slightly clearer in my own mind about my lack of decency." He adds, it makes no sense whatsoever "to theorize about myself."[26] This suggests the ways in which the *Tractatus* may well be considered a war book. In a previous world, ideals would have been better than actuality; in this one, honesty is better than ideals and silence the condition for honesty. Much remains to be said about the language of silence.

Rinaldi is "depressed" by the war, but the same expression was to be used for its surcease. In 1918, Beatrice Webb wrote about the coming post-war world:

> There is little or no elation among the general body of citizens about the coming peace. . . . What are the social ideals germinating in the minds of the five millions who will presently return from the battlefields and battle seas? What is the outlook of the millions of men and women who have been earning high wages and working long hours at the war trades and will presently find themselves seeking work? What are the sympathies of the eight millions of new women voters? The Bolsheviks grin at us from a ruined Russia and their creed, like the plague of influenza, seems to be spreading westwards from one country to another. Will famine become chronic again over whole stretches of Europe, and will some deadly pestilence be generated out of famine to scourge even those races who have a sufficiency of food? Will Western Europe flare up in the flames of anarchic revolution? Individuals brood over these questions and wonder what will have happened this time next year. Hence the depressed and distracted air of the strange medly of soldiers and civilians who throng the thoroughfares of the capital of the victorious Empire.[27]

Webb had a strange political life, and her reputation is now low, but this passage bears comparison to the ending of the first part of *Democracy in America.* Everything in it from Weimar to fascism seems to have come true. Hemingway had the benefit of ten years of historical experience before predating his version of the above.

Frederic Henry may or may not be "depressed" as Rinaldi is, but he labors under the burden of omniscience. Hemingway knows for him and for the reader that the ideals of 1918 will have become politically extinct. Before the shell lands to inflict that fatal wound on the auto-ambulance crew and on American literary criticism, a dialogue has ensued that may be equally damaging. Frederic Henry is arguing tactically against the Socialist idealism of Gavuzzi, Manera, and Passini. But it can be said that both Henry and Hemingway are arguing against any form of political idealism:

> "I believe we should get the war over," I said. "It would not finish it if one side stopped fighting. It would only be worse if we stopped fighting."
>
> "It could not be worse," Passini said respectfully. "There is nothing worse than war."
>
> "Defeat is worse."
>
> I do not believe it," Passini said still respectfully. "What is defeat? You go home."
>
> "They come after you. They take your home. They take your sisters."
>
> "I don't believe it," Passini said. "They can't do that to everybody. Let everybody defend his home. Let them keep their sisters in the house."
>
> "They hang you. They come and make you be a soldier again. Not in the auto-ambulance, in the infantry."
>
> "They can't hang every one."
>
> "An outside nation can't make you be a soldier," Manera said. "At the first battle you all run."
>
> "Like the Tchecos."
>
> "I think you do not know anything about being conquered and so you think it is not bad." (49–50)

This implies the history of Europe from 1920 on, much as Beatrice Webb thought it might be and as Hemingway thought it had turned out. The unspoken answer to the assertion is that they *can* hang everyone. The novel prefigures the police state with its social breakdown, its constant danger of informers, its militarization. Most of all, it implies the end of civilized expectations: this passage is full of our post-war awareness of the violation of taboos and the unimagined violation of limits on power. Unthinkable before, they are now, Hemingway recognizes, part of the assumptions of reality. And this book is above all realistic.

The conditions have been set for fascism. With great political insight Hemingway has weighted the development of fascism against the decline of idealism. The auto-ambulance crew thinks in terms of pre-1914 possibilities. We know where Passini has gotten his ideas—as he puts it, "We think. We read. We are not peasants" (51). He is, in other words, a victim of ideas in circulation. Every assertion that Passini makes comes from the armory of Socialism; every response by Frederic Henry comes from Hemingway's skeptical experience of the twenties in Italy. Fixated on social justice (itself a major irony), the crew is oblivious to reality. Henry is politically astute, but the impact of this exchange is a consequence of the infusion of fact and feeling from the end of the decade. That verifies Henry's *realpolitik*.

Throughout the story men believe that if they stop fighting—if they throw away their rifles—then peace will arrive. More important, if the war is stopped, then life can resume its norms. That life would proceed, as Bertrand Russell described, in a way foretold by late-Victorian idealism: "There was to be ordered progress throughout the world, no revolutions, a gradual cessation of war, and an extension of parliamentary government."[28] It is the issue that Hemingway's omniscience best allows him to unveil. We ought to ask whether, along with the experience of war and of love denied, the novel makes other points, political and even metaphysical. Throughout, men have believed in some kind of public and personal order, and they have developed ideas that William James called remedies for the world of facts. Nearly every one of these remedies turns out to be wrong. Everywhere we see logical but unreal expectations: preparation means victory, victory means peace, peace means order. Throughout, there are dialogues on the impending world after the war—although Catherine, who also has a sense of military history, tells Henry, when he is thinking too far ahead, "Don't worry, darling. We may have several babies before the war is over" (155).

The effect of the war on Catherine Barkley, after her loss at the Battle of the Somme, and on Frederic Henry, after his wound, leads us naturally to conclude that it should be understood in terms of trauma. But Henry has been wounded before the *Minnenwerfer.* In 1915, in the essay that I have previously cited, Freud made his own contribution to the subject. He argued that a new kind of disillusionment would force a new relationship between men, women, and states. Until now, there had been a universal premise: If we lived lives of productive repression, if we accepted "much renunciation of instinctual gratification," then the state also would operate within certain limits. Its own public conscience would tacitly confirm private morals. Our individual lives, in other words, would be reflected, sanctioned, made fully intelligible. The first thing the war proved, however, was that states themselves no longer believed in the denial of aggressive impulses; and if *that* was true, why curb ours? We were bound to have become "disillusioned" because there was no longer any *point* to "high standards of accepted custom for the individual."[29] Public morality led only to war, private morality only to unhappiness. In *A Farewell to Arms* the exercise of the will and the force of conscience do not lead to anything. Toward the end of the novel (327) Hemingway actually invokes the concept of "rules" of life but states that we never have the time to learn them. There is a strong implication that even obeying the "rules" guarantees nothing. That is to say, there is no connection between will, act, and fate. Those are some of the issues on Frederic Henry's mind. He is in some obvious ways a victim of the experience of war, but he is more centrally aware—has from the beginning been aware—that the war has exposed the illusion of order. He knows that the world of James has become that of Freud.

Henry is set apart from most others in this story who fail to recognize that order is both a historical and a philosophical illusion, an idea whose time has gone. Many are looking for an overarching explanation of life through the schemata of religion, science, or politics, but none of these systems holds up. The reason why Hemingway ends this novel in chaos, disorder, and accident is that when these are elevated to the status of principles they make as much sense as their opposites. The novel's antiphilosophy is set against the system-building of the moment, not all of it Fascist. About one system, Hemingway was to put the issue this way: "It isn't all in Marx nor in Engels. . . . A lot of things have happened since then." Political fantasies of the era 1914–29 are answered by this story of personal and of ideological *defeat.* The utopian versions of *hope* in the twenties—Progressive, Socialist, Communist—dictated a Wellsian "perfected future"; however, as Eric Hobsbawm has observed, the twenties finished off the Age of Liberalism, destroying one after another those institutions of democracy that Bertrand Russell among many others took for granted.[30]

A Farewell to Arms is not entirely a war book but a post-war book. We might liken it to Isaiah Berlin's famous analysis of political realism versus idealism: the belief that we can discover *any* "correct, objectively valid solution to the question of how men should live," may, Berlin stated, itself be in "principle not true." So the pursuit of order, whether through science, religion, or politics, is futile by definition.[31] Philosophically and psychologically, Hemingway found nothing that might make imperfect life endurable, and there were no remedies for facts.

8

Hemingway and Experience

Hemingway resisted the idea that writing should primarily restate the facts of experience, identifying that with "photographic plate" journalism, of which he had a low opinion.[1] A next step is required, that of finding—through an act of intellectual conscience—the kind of language that most closely approximates (because it least fails) the truth of perception: One must argue with language in order to produce truth. Nevertheless, there may be inherent limits governing the translation of experience.Carlos Baker's *Hemingway: The Writer as Artist* treats *The Green Hills of Africa* as a study in the reproduction of "experience" through "verisimilitude." In order to accomplish that, the recollection of detail is essential, including every aspect of appearance and particularly sensory impressions. Experience recalled is fidelity to perception. In addition, since the writing deals not only with landscape but also with human change, character and style need also to be implied. Baker warns us, however, that the "unprocessed raw material" of a month in Africa clearly defies restatement because it has no plot. So, there must be a compromise: the book is anchored by its depiction of factual "truth" and made into literature by the imposition of narrative themes like pursuit, rivalry, failure, success.[2]

Hemingway himself wrote in 1935 that the mere accuracy of reporting was useless: "But if you make it up instead of describe it you can make it round and whole and solid and give it life. You create it, for good or bad. It is made; not described."[3] One of the paradoxes of writing about experience was that truth required fiction—and additional complications exist.

Hemingway's stories of the mid-twenties have much to say about the problem of stating experience. One of the most moving of these stories, "The Undefeated," is about a *matador* past his prime and overmatched in his last bullfight. The narrative is also literally about writing. We see an action taking place and simultaneously the way in which it is interpreted. Manuel, the bullfighter, has momentarily regained the style and form of his youth. Against the odds he puts on a heroic and grandly stylistic performance. In one narrative voice we see this happening, but in another we see it degraded. That is because the action is documented as it happens by the substitute bullfight critic of El Heraldo, a hack who is the voice of the mass audience. He cannot understand movement, so he disgorges a simile, and the bull is like a fast car. He cannot understand style, so Manuel looks to him like a diminished Belmonte. He does not really see the picador's horse, so it becomes in his small, echoing mind Don Quixote's Rosinante. The story is in the form of a narration giving us approximate truth, accompanied by a second narration that cannot see, understand, or reconstruct it. The substitute critic—and I think he substitutes for all critics—represents a norm, not an aberration. He is a mechanization of literacy. One implication is that honest writing is an adversary procedure; another, that experience truly recalled is unlikely. There is also the implication that Manuel's relationship to critics is the same as Hemingway's.

In "Soldier's Home" a veteran named Krebs has returned to Oklahoma from the Great War, but there is not much greatness in his condition. He would like to be a hero—possibly he has been—but he cannot compete with other tellers of tales, and he is too alienated to exert his own imagination. So he begins to experiment with fiction: "His lies were quite unimportant lies and consisted in attributing to himself things other men had seen, done or heard of, and stating as facts certain apocryphal incidents familiar to all soldiers. . . . Krebs acquired the nausea in regard to experience that is the result of untruth or exaggeration" (146).[4] Falsification is at first a tactic, but it becomes more dangerous than it seems. It may be that experience is incommunicable, and Krebs, in his limited way, manages to show the essential problem of imagination. The recollection of experience may alter it, whereas its restatement may corrupt it. Language itself becomes problematic, and there is also that "nausea" about experience dishonestly cited, an idea that needs some development.

To move from the statement that "Hemingway based his work on his experience" to the statement that "Hemingway's stories restate experience" is to pass through a fairly complex terrain of philosophy.

Were there debates with which Hemingway might argue? *Knowledge and Experience,* T. S. Eliot's dissertation, reminds us forcibly that the dialogue of the two irreconcilable concepts embedded in its title became part of modernism. F. H. Bradley had stated that reality could be objectively discerned, but Eliot thought that it might not be either discerned or communicated: "All significant truths are private truths." As Lyndall Gordon puts it, "Eliot looked upon the world as a precarious, artificial construction. Divergent images were rather arbitrarily drawn into a frame of common knowledge which was eroded at every moment by fresh subjective experience. Eliot's world was dangerously fragile—poised, like Poe's city in the sea, on the edge of dissolution. It had no permanent substance: it was 'essentially vague, unprecise, swarming with insoluble contradictions.' Yet it tugged. It insisted on acknowledgement." The subject is immense; although Hemingway was deeply aware of Eliot, he was probably more concerned with related aspects of the problem of experience. As for the knowledge part, Wittgenstein had theorized insurmountable obstacles about even understanding it: "Even if *all possible* scientific questions be answered, the problems of life have still not been touched at all." Even if they can be assessed, "whatever we do, we are never sure that we are not mistaken."[5] It would be improbable for Hemingway to have studied Wittgenstein, but it would also have been improbable for him to escape ideas that, from 1922 on, circulated through the intellectual world and contributed to its uncertainties.[6] As to the organization of patterns around the idea of experience, a well-defined summary of possibilities existed: John Dewey's large collection of essays under the heading of *Experience and Nature* undertook to review for the mid-decade audience, ideas about "the doings and undoings that constitute experience." As Dewey sees it, experience is mentally organized around (and may even inherently consist of) polarities, a proposition that corresponds to Carlos Baker's sense of inevitable pattern imposed upon detail: "Structure and process, substance and accident, matter and energy, permanence and flux, one and many, continuity and discreteness, order and progress, law and liberty, uniformity and growth, tradition and innovation, rational will and impelling desires, proof and discovery, the actual and the possible, are names given to various phases of their conjunction, and the issue of living depends upon the art with which these things are adjusted to each other."[7] Dewey asserted a kind of intellectual obligation in speaking of experience: it took place in nature and had to be understood as the interaction between our minds and "stones, plants, animals, diseases, health, temperature, electricity," and all other aspects of nature. And Dewey, who throughout his writing grants that fiction may do a better job than science in describing aspects of life, states axiomatically that "the fact that something is an occurrence does not decide what kind of an occurrence it is; that can be found out only by examination. . . . A bare event is no event at all; *something* happens. What that something is, is found out by actual study." Also in the mid-twenties Dewey put the matter this way: "events are not events" without interpretation. Like Hemingway he thinks that history is by no means the most accurate mode of reconstructing the truth of experience unless it is "brought down close to the actual scene of events."[8]

Dewey wrote about experience with the understanding that more than one point of view was being summarized: he will, for example, cite both religious and secular interpretations. Some points he makes are especially useful for understanding ideas of the mid-twenties. To take one of his essays that shares Hemingway's concerns, experience may well appear to be (and in actuality be) "precarious." Here, as he does habitually, Dewey examines "culture," or what he called the statement of ideas in language. He ranges from anthropology to Grimm's fairy tales in order to flesh out one modern interpretation of life, one that "man finds himself living in an aleatory world; his existence involves, to put it baldly, a gamble. The world is a scene of risk; it is uncertain, unstable, uncannily unstable. Its dangers are irregular, inconstant, not to be counted upon as to their times and seasons." This view matters a great deal, because philosophy, religion, and our conventional wisdom posit something entirely different, a "finished" world of "sufficiencies, tight completeness, order, recurrences which make possible prediction." We make choices, if we can, about which of these worlds we inhabit: experience having both precarious and stable potentialities.[9] Clearly, these are choices made in Hemingway's writings.

Cleanth Brooks wrote about the first of these potentialities in an essay on Hemingway in *The Hidden God,* deriving his thesis too from philosophical debate. He begins by invoking Paul Tillich's *Theology of Culture* and then applies it to the fiction of experience. As Brooks saw the case, it had become almost impossible for "the serious writer" to offer anything real to the "conditioned reflexes" of his culture. Readers expect Book-of-the-Month Club views about life, and in some important ways fiction must correspond to a weltanschauung created by advertisements. Hemingway, unlike other writers in his cultural moment, shows how one actually lives within a precarious universe, endowing it now and then with hard-won stability. Brooks's subject is "A Clean, Well-Lighted Place," and his analysis of it may come from Tillich; but the terminology relates to the debate on order versus instability that James made central to our intellectual lives and that Dewey reinstated. The language that Brooks uses—a "hostile" or "indifferent" universe is shaped into something stable ("orderly and tidy") by an effort of the will—tends, I think, to show that.[10]

Before Tillich absorbed these materials—and certainly before Dewey—philosophy had pondered the desire for order in an unstable world. Dewey, however, brought the issue into the mid-twenties. He admired the ability of fiction to deal with ideas and himself wrote with feeling about the "precarious" (hence novelistic) aspect of experience. He is worth reading for his discussion of the fear that existence entails, resulting in our many "expiations and propitiations." Although we tend to think of Dewey as being almost overpoweringly an agent of stability, he concluded that, "when all is said and done, the fundamentally hazardous character of the world is not seriously modified."[11] That provides a context for the twenties and for Hemingway: "Thinkers are concerned to mitigate the instability of life, to introduce moderation, temper and economy, and when worst comes to worst to suggest consolations and compensations. They are concerned with rendering more stable good things, and more unstable bad things. . . . The facts of the ongoing, unfinished and ambiguously potential world give point and poignancy to the search for absolutes and finalities."[12]

Hemingway had a number of his own choices to make in regard to the interpretation of experience. One choice necessarily involves Protestant and Catholic doctrines. Hemingway's religious life evolved, as Brooks implies, against a complex of explanations. Both the religion he left and that to which he converted each offered to human experience their own Unified Field Theory. Each had their own systematic understanding of those things—despair, age, the chaos of desire—against which any theology of order had to poise itself. We know the limited success of such views in *A Farewell to Arms.*[13] They do not have a great deal of persuasive power, and the dialogues concerning them take place within scenes of failed persuasion.

A second set of choices derived from that American idealism which is for us an atmospheric condition. This choice was clearly impossible for Hemingway—bad enough to be confined to religious explanation, but worse to have the same kind of explanation appear in secular form.

A third set of choices centered on the naturalistic interpretation of experience. This confronts the emotional and intellectual falsity of hope, always balanced against the facts and probabilities of experience. One of Hemingway's most allusive endings refers itself to that opposition:

> We sat close against each other. I put my arm around her and she rested against me comfortably. It was very hot and bright, and the houses looked sharply white. We turned out onto the Gran Via.
>
> "Oh, Jake," Brett said, "we could have had such a damned good time together."
>
> Ahead was a mounted policeman in khaki directing traffic. He raised his baton. The car slowed suddenly pressing Brett against me.
>
> "Yes." I said. "Isn't it pretty to think so?" (247)[14]

The end phrase has been the subject of a thoughtful essay by Earl Rovit in which he discussed the "policy of exclusion" in Hemingway. Hemingway's last six words seem far too brief to explain anything directly, yet they communicate important ideas. For one thing, they make us aware of "the studied impersonality of what is not said."[15] That in itself is a Hemingway technique—but it is also a philosophy. I hope to develop these points; meanwhile, I note of this ending line its implication that experience differs from its interpretation; that we are unwilling to concede the point; that Brett, who is being addressed, is customarily deluding and possibly delusive; that precarious reality is here and probably in general disguised as if it were potentially stable; and that emotional experience is difficult to state in any appropriate language. Hence that word "pretty" used by Jake, which gives Brett's sentiment ("we could have had such a damned good time together") exactly the kind of lightness of being that it signifies and also requires in response.

Hemingway states many of his important points in the form of unanswered questions, some of which are unanswerable, others which have too many answers. Dewey had by 1924 reminded readers that ambiguity (not notably important as an American intellectual style) was nevertheless a characteristic of life. When pursued as an idea it led ineluctably to the conclusion that our experience was extremely difficult to decipher. It might, in fact, be chaotic: it is only our *thinking* (not necessarily accurate) that transforms "the disordered into the orderly, the mixed-up into the distinguished or placed, the unclear and ambiguous into the defined and unequivocal, the disconnected into the systematized."[16] Jake Barnes understands the daily necessity of reinterpreting the world against the evidence, making it stable rather than precarious. "Moderation," "temper," and "economy" are words Dewey found useful to summarize the "stable" point of view, and they are also useful for our understanding of Jake Barnes who deploys them against the experiential odds. *They seem to be traits of character only, but are of course ways of forcing stability on a world that really is precarious.* When Jake exerts these qualities in personal life, he participates also in a much larger script about men and women in nature and among themselves. As to that condition, one understands that while he is an agency of order in *The Sun Also Rises,* order is only momentary. The condition is inherently ambiguous: he makes Brett happy while losing Montoya's respect, knowing that the happiness will be temporary, whereas the loss of respect will be permanent. Not much in his world can be said to be "defined and unequivocal."

~

Hemingway is concerned with two related problems, telling the truth, and staying silent about it. The former was raised in the correspondence with Max Perkins over the manuscript version of *A Farewell to Arms* in 1929. Perkins wrote that there was too much truth in Catherine's death scene, and he argued for "reducing the physical detail." Both Perkins and Owen Wister had concluded that "the physical aspects of the affair are too intensely presented," that Hemingway had succeeded in creating horror and suffering beyond the power of his audience to appreciate. This went far beyond the censorship of four-letter words in the text, and Hemingway tried to explain that in creating suffering, he had also created "truth."[17] He did modify the text in many ways; however, possibly more interesting is that at other times, he had reservations about the communication of "truth."

Nevertheless, "truth" may not be as directly connected to communication as it may appear. A letter to Perkins about the hurricane of 1935 in the Florida Keys has one of the great mordant passages in Hemingway: "Max, you can't imagine it. two women, naked, tossed up into the trees by the water, swollen and stinking, their breasts as big as balloons flies between their legs. Then, by figuring, you locate where it is and recognize them as the two very nice girls who ran a sandwich place and fillingstation three miles from the ferry. We located sixty nine bodies where no one had been able to get in. Indian Key absolutely swept clean, not a blade of grass, and over the high center of it were scattered live conchs that came in with the sea, craw fish, and dead morays. The whole bottom of the sea blew over it."[18] As we know from "A Natural History of the Dead," "the sight of a dead woman is quite shocking," and we are meant first to be shocked out of our existential complacency (441). The point of the passage is the *natural* inversion of what has seemed all along to be a *natural* sequence: from clothed to naked, from alive to dead, from the human to the organic, from breathing air to breathing water, all without a map. There are two versions of the idea of nature: the idealist expectation of order and sequence and its more probable opposite, the chaos of experience. The language of explanation that ensues, however, makes for a large problem—one not unforeseen by a writer who distrusted political dogma. The letter, like Hemingway's article in *The New Masses,* written at the same time (September 1935), tries to find a reason for everything experienced; it blames first the Miami Weather Bureau that failed to warn of the storm, then a train that might have transported people to safety had it left on time, and then Harry Hopkins and FDR for being part of an uncaring government; and there is blame in reserve for ambitious, rivalrous, aspiring writers on storms and undertakers who profit from them. The letter and article are brilliant agitprop. At this point in Hemingway's intellectual life there are explanations for fate. The writing is still superb, but recollecting "experience" now means finding political reasons for it. So, the details are as finely envisioned as ever, but the narrative is unconvincing.[19]

The "nausea" of experience was restated a decade after "Soldier's Home" in "The Snows of Kilimanjaro," at the point where Harry thinks about stories he will never write. But in the midst of the passage, after one of the most brilliant descriptions of experience Hemingway or anyone else ever resurrected (itself a stunner of a paradox), there is the statement, "he could not talk about it or stand to have it mentioned" (66). This kind of silence recurs throughout the fiction. In *A Farewell to Arms,* Rinaldi cannot talk about what he knows, and Frederic Henry cannot bear to hear about experience that has been sanctified by sanctimonious discourse. Hemingway's work has many moments when language falsifies experience, and it cannot be trusted or used. His writing of the twenties displays, at any given time, a kind of Gresham's Law of language in operation.

The issue is not, I think, about what Jake Barnes calls "unexplained horrors" (167) when he explains the bullfight to Brett. If anything, Hemingway argues *for* bringing such things to consciousness, just as he had argued against the marketplace instincts of Perkins and Owen Wister. It may be that the recollection of experience involves taboo and that we should refer the subject to Frazer and to Freud. Hemingway, I think, felt it to be more than philosophically important to keep a kind of silent faith with the moment. Part of his endless series of rituals, as in "Big Two-Hearted River," is keeping silence about experience, being satisfied by the idea of the "mysterious" because the connection to nature is so easily broken and falsified by discourse.

When Wittgenstein wrote about Frazer, he suggested that rituals were not in fact *intellectually* primitive: tribes did not try to produce rain in the dry season because they knew it to be impossible. They wanted only to acknowledge that rain was essential to life.[20] Hemingway clearly disagreed: ritual does matter because of the connection it establishes between mind and nature. Reason alone is insufficient. This often puzzles critics, but the conception is in fact more convincing than, say, Conrad's account of Kurtz in the Congo, that part of *Heart of Darkness* in which savage ritual appeals only because it is savage and not ritual.

Language is usually thought of as the bridge to experience, but it is also a kind of corruption of experience. According to Wittgenstein, language "sets everyone the same traps; it is an immense network of easily accessible wrong turnings."[21] This problem with language may be the central difficulty recognized by Hemingway. Moments of suppression in his fiction cause silence about experience and feeling because language is not to be trusted. This is especially true of the tortured relationships of *The Sun Also Rises*. When Jake tries to convince Brett to live with him (55), she says intelligently, "Let's not talk. Talking's all bilge." There are many implications, although decorum is not one of them. She understands that what she actually experiences sexually with other men can only be approached, and from a vast distance, by the phrasing of "It's the way I'm made." That phrase interpolates a helpfully useless abstraction, i.e., language that prevents access to experience, and it thereby illustrates what all talk is. "Talk" itself is an immense problem for the two of them: Jake says that "when I'm low I talk like a fool" (56). The meaning elegantly reverses what Brett has just said: if language *could* express experience, then it might be useless also, because statement about the experience of feeling is inherently nonrational; and since it states, it also invites chaos. Later, the count enters, and the word "talk" keeps reiterating itself. Two kinds of meaning are implied when he asks Brett to stop drinking—"Why don't you just talk" (58)—and she answers that she talks too much already and has talked herself out with Jake. Following the dialogue, which is about dialogue, is like watching a tennis match on fast-forward. The count is not a fool and is able to follow implied meanings, as when he looks at Brett's empty champagne glass and says that "You don't want to mix emotions up with a wine like that" (59). It makes no sense to confuse idea or impression with actuality.

The count is interesting in this scene because he (literally) embodies a metaphor, refusing to reveal essence, only surface:

> Below the line where his ribs stopped were two raised white welts. "See on the back where they come out." Above the small of the back were the same two scars, raised as thick as a finger.
>
> "I say. Those are something."
>
> "Clean through."
>
> The count was tucking in his shirt.
>
> "Where did you get those?" I asked.
>
> "In Abyssinia. When I was twenty-one years old."
>
> "What were you doing?" asked Brett. "Were you in the army?"
>
> "I was on a business trip, my dear." (60)

Brett immediately recognizes him as "one of us," but not because he has lead a dangerous life. He is one of those who suppress "talk" because it can only compromise the authenticity of experience. There is a moral element to his silence, although not to his experience. The refusal to elaborate is a way of stating the way things seem to be—and possibly are—without the intervention of falsified consciousness.[22]

The count and Ludwig Wittgenstein are an odd conjunction, but both agree that in certain cases one can only describe and not explain. It may be that even description is too untrustworthy to pursue, and we can only refer to something anterior to it: When the count is pushed by Brett to disclose himself, he says, "I have been around very much. I have been around a very great deal" (59). Here is Jake evading an issue:

> "Yes." I said. "I like to do a lot of things."
> "What do you like to do?'
> "Oh," I said, "I like to do a lot of things." (246)

This at the end of the novel might seem disruptively laconic—why is the text moving in circles?—except for its relationship to ideas. Jake is by no means being offhand. He understands from the beginning that very little can be explained because feeling experienced is not necessarily feeling expressed. So, this statement is repeated but refuses to explain itself, having both immediate and representative value. Immediate because he can hide the truth rather than state what can only be an approximation of it, and representative because what he does within this case is related to what he must do outside the case. Most important, he does not have to lie, which is what happens whenever experience is translated.

Can it be translated at all? "Actual" experience, according to Whitehead, is a "flux of perceptions, sensations, and emotions. . . . It is for each person a *continuum,* fragmentary, and with elements not clearly differentiated." And, he added, "I insist on the radically untidy, ill-adjusted character of the fields of actual experience."[23] That being given, the assessment of experience is necessarily cautionary: one does not immediately write down a response to it. In Hemingway, characters continually advise each other not to state what they believe to be feelings, or even facts.

Experience can be silenced, or when raised from the deep, it can be put into some approximating language. But experience is resistant and even inimical to language. So far as Hemingway was concerned, it was useless to try to reconstruct feeling or idea when their transmission leads nowhere. It might even be said, as at Montoya's (131), that "It would not do to expose it to people who would not understand." At the end (243), Brett repents, "let's never talk about it," and Hemingway's major figures assert their honesty—Rinaldi to Frederic Henry, Brett to Jake, and he to her—by refusing to state. Again at Montoya's (132), in order to assert feeling and belief, language itself must be discarded: "there was no password, no set questions that could bring it out." Understanding is reached "without . . . ever saying anything."

Hemingway's text repeats the problem set by the writer to himself, that of translating experience. Like good novelists themselves, his characters reject statement in conventional use and all it represents. The last word belongs to Jake in the last chapter (245): "You'll lose it if you talk about it." The statement alludes to the many silences of the novel—and also to a central theme of modernism. Wittgenstein states in 1930 that the self is implicated in the false translation of feeling and experience: "Each of the sentences I write is trying to say the whole thing, i.e., the same thing over and over again; it is as though they were all simply views of one object seen from different angles." Silence in *The Sun Also Rises* is self-imposed. There can be no use in trying to explain something to others that is opaque to one's self, and in any case "talk" is unsuited to the task. Wittgenstein continues, "when you bump against the limits of your own honesty it is as though your thoughts get into a whirlpool, an infinite regress: You can *say* what you like, it takes you no further."[24] This philosophical sensibility accounts for the restraint so often mentioned—and admired—in Hemingway's works. The issue is not that his figures are without language: they understand that its misuse affects one of the few things left to them, intellectual honor.

The other aspect of this issue is public. Allan Janik and Stephen Toulmin state in their study of Wittgenstein that there is a silent context for all philosophical and literary statement: "In coming to understand what a truly honest valuation is and ought to be, when arrived at with an eye to the very highest standards, we learn also to distinguish it from those other, more slipshod, insincere, or thoughtless expressions of approval or disgust which so often pass for value judgments." Genuine "aesthetic values" or moral values (as Frederic Henry comes to understand) become impossible to realize.[25] Silence in Wittgenstein and in Hemingway signifies resistance to language and its public content.

In *A Farewell to Arms* virtually every major dialogue resists cultural politics through stubborn and honest and unprofitable subjectivity. The war is a useful catalyst, but the book is not about the horrors of war. The integrity of Catherine and of Frederic Henry is a variable of their resistance to conventional wisdoms. That resistance is a theme in Dewey and Russell as well as Wittgenstein. In the case of the latter, Marjorie Perloff has shown how it arises from the experience of war. She writes that, "*Schwäfeln*—the high-minded babble on this or that subject, the insistence on speaking about that of which *one cannot speak*—could itself become a fascinating subject for philosophical/poetical investigation."[26] The conflict of private and public voices is visibly within *The Sun Also Rises,* which resists throughout its text the statement of feeling or the restatement of experience. Both may be—will be—affected by falsities inherent in their translation. *A Farewell to Arms* is particularly attentive to Schwäfeln, as in the long dialogue in which the fascistic Ettore reconstructs the details of his heroism:

> "You're a great boy, Ettore," Mac said. "But I'm afraid you're a militarist."
>
> "I'll be a colonel before the war's over," Ettore said.
>
> "If they don't kill you."
>
> "They won't kill me." He touched the stars at his collar with his thumb and forefinger. "See me do that? We always touch our stars if anybody mentions getting killed. . . . Don't worry about me. I don't drink and I don't run around. I'm no boozer and whorehound. I know what's good for me. . . . I don't have to wait to be promoted. I'm going to be a captain for merit of war. You know. Three stars with the crossed swords and crown above. That's me." (123–24)

Ettore has the mechanical quality of describing his ambitions and his experience from the point of view of someone outside himself. And he is indeed a construct of the larger society to which he is attuned. He keeps on stating his own meaning, but he never seems (as Wittgenstein foresaw of this kind of analysis) to get it right. Both Catherine and Freud seem to agree that the attitude Ettore represents (he likes wound stripes better than medals) may well be an "impediment to civilization."[27] His current wound—"it stinks all the time" (122)—argues a symbolic affliction.

Janik and Toulmin argue that before Wittgenstein, there was far too much readiness to apply theory or interpretation to "real life." After Wittgenstein, "real life" was understood to be in many ways opposed to public life and social life and to the analysis of philosophy itself. As

Wittgenstein phrased it, experience is a matter of "our pulses," and the imposition of ideas does not necessarily clarify experience. Part of the format of modernism is the idea that "*The limits of my language* mean the limits of my world." What is important about statement, and rarely if ever accomplished, is to have it describe "the *essence* of the thing."[28] Language may enable, but it is just as likely to prevent enabling. That is especially true of public language.

For a novelist whose realism is validated by dialogue, Hemingway accomplishes his effect often through silence. But the silence depends on a large and complex set of inferences about statement, and these must be in each case imagined. When Jake Barnes refuses to state what he is thinking, he displays a new attitude toward the authenticity of the subjective and the improbability of communicating its experience. In the case of Frederic Henry, true statement exists not of itself but against false statement. Well before Orwell began to write about language and politics, Hemingway understood their connection. Actual public statement had by 1917 made language in some ways unusable: Lord Northcliffe had reported from the Western Front to the mass audience that "the open-air life, the regular and plenteous feeding, the exercise and the freedom from care and responsibility, keep the soldiers extraordinarily fit and contented." The truth is that the trenches were open graves. There were unimaginable casualties and ways of dying, yet Lloyd George had stated that the typical British soldier enjoyed the war as a game and "died a good sportsman." An article in the *Daily Mirror* reported that British corpses on the Front looked so "quietly faithful" and "steadfast" (epic diction gone rotten), that there could be no doubt how pleased they were to be dead.[29] But, who could have done the looking?

Given the propaganda of writers like H. G. Wells, Arnold Bennett, and Gilbert Murray, as well as politicians, there was an oppositional meaning in silence. Hemingway on political certainty seems to me to be no different than Wittgenstein on certainty's other forms.

In describing experience in both of his novels of the twenties, Hemingway conveys the hostility of the subjective life toward its public context. The following passage works well when Wittgenstein's name is replaced by that of Jake Barnes—or Ernest Hemingway: "One could wash one's hands of communal affairs entirely. Society would go to hell in its own way. All the individual could do was try, like Wittgenstein, to live in his own high-minded way, maintaining and exemplifying in his life his own exacting standards of humanity, intellectual honesty, craftsmanship and personal integrity."[30] In the cases of both men, failure is to be expected.

9

Hemingway's Questions

Throughout Hemingway's work is the evidence of his interest in both religious and secular dogma. "Soldier's Home" is about the social gospel of the early twenties; *The Sun Also Rises* deals not only with Catholicism but also with Robert Cohn's vague and wistful philosophy of self-change; *A Farewell to Arms* begins with the advice of a priest to Frederic Henry on the good life and ends with the denial of existential meanings. *A Farewell to Arms* may be said to debate the conflicted nature of things, raising questions that do not have answers.

By 1929, a matrix had been constructed for such questions. Bertrand Russell, Ludwig Wittgenstein, and Alfred North Whitehead had begun to rethink the idea of conventional systematic explanation. They had been preceded by William James, whose *Pragmatism* undercut the inherently religious impulse to unify ideas, provide causes, unify social life. Hemingway's work is in some ways a mirror of this kind of thought. If the following had been asked of Hemingway, it might have made perfect critical sense: Why did he "find it necessary, in his writings between 1925 and 1933, to rethink the whole problem of religion and God, and why was he able to do so?"[1] His probable answer also would have made critical sense: to rethink the idea of intelligibility and order in life and in fiction. The question was directed to Alfred North Whitehead, and the period corresponds to that between *The Sun Also Rises* and "A Clean, Well-Lighted Place."

Whitehead's Lowell Institute Lectures for 1925 and 1926 became

Science and the Modern World and *Religion in the Making,* essential parts of our intellectual tradition. One subject was the loss of both religious and secular conviction. Whitehead expressed the hope that we lived in a universe of "intelligible relations," but it might be a succession of "bare facts" irreducible to meanings.[2] He echoed William James and Josiah Royce, both of whom had written on the will to believe, which found itself in conflict with a new "radical skepticism" to which they sometimes found themselves sympathetic.[3] As Royce put it, uneasily, certain aspects of religious tradition were clearly "unessential accidents." But the rest mattered, and the public philosophers from the beginning of the century to the end of the twenties attempted, pessimistically, to bridge the material and the spiritual.

One great motive was to provide an underpinning for social order. As Whitehead put it, however, any theory of an understandable life collided with our raw experience of "the facts of the world." Those facts that he named ("physical suffering, mental suffering") are novelistic as well as philosophical subjects.[4] Whitehead's bias was to interpret the "pain" of life (a term he invoked repeatedly) as a form of evil; yet a novelist might react to its cause differently, seeing that cause, not as malign fate but as naturalistic probability—a characteristic of human life rather than an exception to it.

In any case, the path taken by Whitehead was representative of his generation of philosophers: he identified the problems of a world without a convincing moral order—a world of pain and human degradation, a world without explanation. Explanatory systems do not in fact explain "the nature of things as disclosed in our own immediate present experience." We need what Whitehead called faith in reason to interpret such experience. He agreed with William James that few "general principles" could be applied to the "irreducible and stubborn facts" of our lives. Whitehead, like Dewey, hoped that "fragmentary" human experience could be related to something outside itself and also that science would be the vehicle for that. We cannot, however, easily identify any "harmony of logical rationality" governing our acts and ideas.[5] That, Whitehead suggested, was a central issue for "modern minds" in the mid-twenties. Clearly, religious thought had been first and most severely affected. Traditional explanation had gone the way of all flesh: "'My generation,' wrote Dewey's colleague, James H. Tufts,'has seen the passing of systems of thought which had reigned since Augustus. The conception of the world as a kingdom ruled by God, subject to his laws and their penalties, which had been undisturbed by the Protestant Reformation, has dissolved.' "[6]

The dissolution of orthodoxy, however, was by no means a simple process. By the end of the twenties, many of the systems replacing it were themselves replaced. Religion may have lost to Darwin, Marx, Comte, and Spencer, but the successor beliefs in turn also became lost orthodoxies. That is part of the context of *A Farewell to Arms,* and it accounts for much of Hemingway's suspicion of revolutionary dogmas.

As a writer and in *propria persona* Hemingway had a fine eye for intellectual innocence. Jake Barnes and Frederic Henry have much to say about the varieties of idealist explanation. In Hemingway, religious idealism is no more a fiction than socialism, anarchism, or the Wellsian "science" of progress. The intersection of Victorianism and modernism can be seen in the following from Eric Hobsbawm: Having assumed that "the study of human society was a positive science like any other evolutionary discipline from geology to biology," it might well appear "perfectly natural for an author to write a study of the conditions of progress under the title *Physics and Politics, Or thoughts on the application of the principles of 'natural selection' and 'inheritance' to political society.*"[7] That title represents a contradiction to cosmology, but perhaps not a difference.

My own sense of Hemingway's dilemma, caught between equally fallacious interpretations of human character and fate, has been provided by Isaiah Berlin who has especially in his essay on "Vico's Concept of Knowledge" articulated the impossibility of systematically accounting for experience. That last, I think, matters greatly in *A Farewell to Arms,* in which an enormous amount of intellectual energy is expended on what Berlin calls explaining the world to oneself. Here is Berlin on the manifold impositions of the idea of order:

> Conscious effort, deliberate attempts to explain the world to oneself, to discover oneself in it, to obtain from it what one needs and wants, to adapt means to ends, to express one's vision

> or describe what one sees or feels or thinks, individually or collectively. . . . omits too much: unconscious and irrational 'drives,' which even the most developed and trained psychological methods cannot guarantee to lay bare; the unintended and unforeseen consequences of our acts, which we cannot be said to have 'made' if making entails intention; the play of accident; the entire natural world by interaction with which we live and function, which remains opaque inasmuch as it is not, *ex hypothesi,* the work of our hands or mind; since we do not 'make' this, how can anything it possesses be grasped as *verum*? How can there be a *scienza* of such an amalgam?[8]

And, Berlin asks, what can the relationship possibly be between Vico's Catholic orthodoxy and his "anthropological, linguistic, historical naturalism?"[9] That may be a useful question for Hemingway.

~

The *Oxford English Dictionary* states that "dialogue" is, as we might expect, dramatic speech, and it also notes that dialogue is an essential form for the interchange of thought. Hemingway used the form in both senses, and especially in the sense of one of its submeanings, as a mode of philosophical inquiry. The dialogue of questioning begins with Plato, continues through Hume—with many stops in between—and survives as the rhetorical questioning of reader by writer in the Public Philosophy. It resurfaces in the work of Hemingway, who uses the mode with great precision and with considerable fidelity to the patterns established by philosophy. His interlocutors ask questions that seem to be as ordinary as those of Socrates, but they demand answers that baffled James, Dewey, and Whitehead. As I have suggested in writing about "The Killers," Hemingway's questions move quickly from the ordinary circumstances of daily life to much larger issues behind them. Nick and George want to know what "it's all about," that is, what is happening, while the real issue is why is it happening—and what does it mean?

There is a group of such questions in "Indian Camp," ranging from things that can be stipulated or even quantified ("Where are we going?"

[92]) to things so far from definition ("Is dying hard?" [95]) that it is difficult even to frame a rational response.[10] There are over fifty questions in "The Killers" whose essential task is, I think, unsentimentally to deny Dewey's supposition (and that of many others) that "we live in a world replete with meaning, a world with an organic unity of some kind."[11] "A Clean, Well-Lighted Place" has harder questions and a number of complex inferences about them. For example, the terminology it uses—"nothing," "despair"—conjoins disparate meanings in no less a way than metaphysical poetry. These terms may be used by two waiters unaware of philosophical allusiveness, but they refer themselves to much larger forms of themselves.

A Farewell to Arms is a special case because it has in its stichomythic dialogues more questions than can be easily formulated or even tabulated. Its characters insistently question each other, and some of their questions may not have determinant limits. Many of the questions invite answers in addition to and different from those stipulated. That is part of the novel's strategy. The idea of "questioning" itself becomes a paradigm. Here is one of the central episodes on the bank of the Tagliamento:

> "If you are going to shoot me," the lieutenant-colonel said, "please shoot me at once without further questioning. The questioning is stupid. . . . "
>
> I heard the shots. They were questioning some one else. This officer. . . . cried when they read the sentence from the pad of paper, and they were questioning another when they shot him. They made a point of being intent on questioning the next man while the man who had been questioned before was being shot. . . . I did not know whether I should wait to be questioned.[12] (224)

A first response to this concludes, probably rightly, that the end of the procedure has the same relationship to justice that the experience of the procedure has to meaning. One will be drawn instinctively to Kafka and his nameless interlocutors. But Hemingway has his own interrogative mode, and when his prose economy is interrupted by so many repetitions of "questioning," we may be intended to see the term in a more than cognitive way. There is in fact a thirteen-term sequence in this episode of "questioning," "questioned," and "questioners" (the cited passage contains only half of them). We hear many of the questions and also answers to them. The page of text is of course punctuated with question marks, which has its own effect. Some of the questions—"Regiment?"—can be answered with the kind of linguistic precision that even Wittgenstein might accept. That particular question suggests limits of interpretation. It also implies that other questions have the same kinds of precise answers; however, other questions, such as, "Why are you not with your regiment?" (223), suggest an impossible compression of experience into language. Only a Hemingway or Tolstoy could provide the answer, and one of them has just tried. To hear that question after experiencing the retreat from Caporetto is to understand not only the beginnings of fascism but also the mindset that made fascism possible. Clearly, the issue involves much more than pedantic brutality. By the time we have gone through interrogation with the lieutenant-colonel and Frederic Henry, we understand that there is no answer that will satisfy the questions. Reasoning itself is undesired, inferior to political mythology. We are meant to extrapolate.

Questioning is a paradigm in this novel, but its questions have different orders of magnitude. Some are about ultimate meanings: what life is, how and why it ends, whether it has a discernible plot. These are the famous questions of the ending, of the multiple unused endings. They are expressed through monologues. Others, more mundane but not less interesting, are expressed through dialogues. When Hemingway considers and rejects traditional idealist and new materialist solutions, he relies necessarily on a context. And the great context of his time was the problem of accounting for our experience of the world by means of religious, materialist, or positivist explanation of that experience. As far as that range of explanation was concerned, Bertrand Russell, in a book also published in 1929, argued for "logical atomism" or "verifiable results" instead of for exploded generalizations. He wanted a descriptive and mathematical model of reality, and he did not believe that such was possible in a world deluded by religious dogma.[13]

Hemingway had a good deal of company in his own concern for "abstract words" (185) with exploded meanings. Some of those words trailed clouds of metaphysical glory, claiming an answer for everything personal or political. But they did not come close to having answers to his particular questions, or to those of contemporary philosophy. William James had already dismissed "all the great single-word answers to the world's riddle, such as God, the One, Reason, Law, Spirit, Matter, Nature, Polarity, the Dialectic Process, the Idea, the Self, the Oversoul," and he was to be followed by Lippmann in the next generation.[14] Dewey was to lecture in 1925 and 1926 about the gilding of politics with religious values, anticipating Hemingway's coverage of the subject: "the words 'sacred' and 'sanctity'. . . . testify to the religious aureole which protects . . . institutions. If 'holy' means that which is not to be approached nor touched, save with ceremonial precautions and by specially anointed officials, then such things are holy in contemporary political life. As supernatural matters have progressively been left high and dry upon a secluded beach, the actuality of religious taboos has more and more gathered about secular institutions, especially those connected with the nationalistic state."[15] *A Farewell to Arms* records that false effect or "aureole" designed to impose political upon existential meanings. The "sacred" is the subject of a number of dialogues in Hemingway's novel, as when Frederic Henry states that he "had seen nothing sacred" (185) about dying in the war, or at least nothing that could adequately be explained by its apologists. There is a moment of deconstructive comedy in the episode I have cited, when the battle police on the Tagliamento accuse him of betraying "the sacred soil of the fatherland" (223). The point is, we have until this invocation experienced "the sacred soil"—in the form of mud and dirt—intensively: Our milieu has been trench mud, wet dirt, ambulance-swallowing quicksand, "brush and mud" (205), and an infinite amount of potentially sacred dust on the roads leading to the battlefield. We have choked in that soil, been drowned in it by explosives; and so much of it has blown into Henry's wound that it has prevented hemorrhage. You cannot escape the soft and muddy sacred soil, which is why the ambulance has finally to be abandoned on the retreat from Caporetto and why life of one kind has to end and another begin. Terminology is often false, whereas the relationship of false ideals to actuality is implied by Gino's observation (deadpan comedy is the right mode) that "the soil is sacred. . . . But I wish it grew more potatoes" (184).

Russell wrote about the falsified relationships of a highly significant moment: "there was another problem which began to interest me at about the same time—that is to say, about 1917. This was the problem of the relation of language to facts." It was "the essential function of words to have a connection of one sort or another with facts." But "the superstitious view of language" insists on endowing facts with "awe" and mystery. Russell argued at length that although it was impossible for language ever to be universally true, it should aim for precision, and it should be descriptive toward that end.[16]

In 1922, in the introduction to Wittgenstein's *Tractatus,* Russell had this to say not only of the idea of accurate statement but of the philosophical trend of the decade: "The essential business of language is to assert or deny facts. . . . In order that a certain sentence should assert a certain fact there must, however the language may be constructed, be something in common between the structure of the sentence and the structure of the fact. This is perhaps the most fundamental thesis of Mr. Wittgenstein's theory."[17] Substantially more is involved, however: Marjorie Perloff writes of the conclusion of the *Tractatus* ("Whereof one cannot speak, thereof one must be silent") that it "is no more than the commonsense recognition that there are metaphysical and ethical aporias that no discussion, explication, rationale, or well-constructed argument can fully rationalize."[18] This puts another slant on Frederic Henry's impatience with the language of assertion.

The language given to Frederic Henry by Hemingway would if possible confine itself to number, date, and place: "There were many words that you could not stand to hear and finally only the names of places had dignity. Certain numbers were the same way and certain dates" (185). To say more of these things, as politicians or generals do, is to aggrandize one's self by corrupting meanings. In this novel and at that moment, language itself is a field of contention. Political and religious dogma now define meanings, and no explanation can itself be exempt from questioning. In discussing Wittgenstein, Marjorie Perloff states the vital importance of *description.* The refusal to explain is, I think, an echo of Wittgenstein's refusal to accept imposed meanings or to invent new ones too easily: "one can only *describe* and say: this is what human life is like."[19] Throughout *A Farewell to Arms* is a consistent refusal to endow fact with meaning, expressed either by Frederic Henry's not resonating emotionally to accepted meanings, ignoring them, or exploding certainties through strategic questioning. The priest tries to elicit some emotional commitment from Henry, but the answer is simply, "If I ever get it I will tell you" (72). Catherine understands the meanings of her dreams about the rain but refuses (126) to discuss them because knowledge cannot do anything about them; Count Greffi says about his explanation of the war that he may as well quote "the examples on the other side" (262) of the case. As in the famous passage on the language of the "sacred" and "glorious" (184–85), this attitude can become explicit, otherwise the text itself denies amplification. Silence is the ultimate answer to fake explanation and to the assumption that reason prevails.

A long dialogue between Rinaldi and Frederic Henry conveys a good deal more than narrative information; it makes certain points about experience as against the consciousness and restatement of experience. The polarities are conventional idealism and, against that, the modernist attitude formulated by Wittgenstein. Neither man's experience is reified by dialogue. In fact, the opposite is true, because there must be resistance to what can be stated about what can be known or felt. First, explanation is itself futile as an intellectual enterprise. According to Rinaldi, "I know many things I can't say" (170). He means, I think, not that the decencies of conversation impose limits on discourse but that statement about knowledge, feeling, or experience is necessarily dishonest as compared with experience itself. What Dewey found uplifting, Wittgenstein found embarrassing. It is at least cautionary for the present, in which our own confidence in the therapeutic revelation of self is intellectually embarrassing—and also useless.

Rinaldi states that "we all start complete" and "never get anything new" (171) and that there is no use whatever in "thinking so much" about ultimate meanings. Facts impose meanings. Rinaldi in 1917 seems to have been reading Wittgenstein in 1929: Existence "cannot be expressed in the form of a question, nor is there any answer to it." The attempt to frame questions and answers may simply be a "running up against the limits of language." Moreover, what we do know, "we know a priori," without the mediation of systems. There is only "the totality of facts" in the experienced world, a fact that in itself presupposes Frederic Henry's dispassionate connection to his world. Wittgenstein scholars draw a particularly clear distinction between "representational description," which is inherently suited for facts, and the more difficult and unclear language of values.[20]

The assertion of empirical truth (so far as it can go) over systematic falsehood is characteristic of *A Farewell to Arms.* Michael Reynolds draws a distinction between "the life of the spirit" and the opposed "life of the flesh" in the novel, and clearly the former has failed.[21] In his unwillingness to accept providential explanation, Hemingway shares the empiricism newly enforced on philosophies. But the same skepticism applies to secular answers for disputed questions. *A Farewell to Arms* may break as many secular as religious icons.

Hemingway placed some of the most disturbing moments in the novel in identifiably secular contexts. They involve politics and ideology. There are, for example, few lines more graphic than Bonello's "all my life I've wanted to kill a sergeant" (207). Not an unknown response for those in the military—but strange to have that wish *before* serving. Bonello does not mind admitting this in confession, because that is in another realm and politically unserious. But he and the others from Imola reserve their own beliefs:

> "Are you all socialists?"
> "Everybody."
> "Is it a fine town?"
> "Wonderful. You never saw a town like that."
> "How did you get to be socialists?"
> "We're all socialists. Everybody is a socialist. We've always been socialists."
> "You come, Tenente, We'll make you a socialist too." (208)

It is not strange to find socialists in 1917 in Imola or anywhere else. The strangeness, and it is considerable, comes from the contrast between two phrases, "all my life" and "we've always been."

The core doctrine of socialism was, of course, even by 1917—

especially in 1917—the secularized version of brotherhood. In that year, H. G. Wells, whom Hemingway has planted in *A Farewell to Arms,* sent his letter of "fraternal support" to Maxim Gorky for "this struggle to liberate mankind . . . and to establish international goodwill on the basis of international justice and respect."[22] In Hemingway, the idea provides a backboard for skepticism. Revolution and reform interest him because of their internal orthodoxies and contradictions. For example, Bonello runs away like the sergeant he has executed for running away—although Piani stays, because, as he says to Henry, "I did not want to leave you" (217). The events of the retreat tend to invalidate not only hopes but ideas. There is a deep resistance of facts to their ordering, as in "The Capital of the World" in which a parlor revolutionary states that "only through the individual can you attack the class. It is necessary to kill the individual bull and the individual priest. All of them. Then there are no more." But he is told to shut up and "save it for the meeting" (42). Work is, after all, better than canned politics. The revolutionist accuses his friend of being fatally lukewarm, but in Hemingway, to say that "you lack all ideology" is no insult but high praise: "*Mejor si me falta eso que el otro.*"

The Bonello dialogue is a reprise of one earlier with Manera, Gavuzzi, and Passini. Frederic Henry's brutal political wisdom is set against their socialist idealism. That idealism has its religious equivalents in more than one sense of the term, as when Passini says unhopefully, "We will convert him" (51). These men still believe that soldier-workers should stop fighting for merely national interests; that "there is a class that controls a country" whose members "make money" out of the war; and that "war is not won by victory."[23] These are words unrelated to facts. Frederic Henry tells Passini "you're an orator"—but that is definitely not praise. We will later be told of Henry's contempt for all those "shouted words . . . proclamations. . . . abstract words" (185) that are political lies. The significance of the *Minnenwerfer* that arrives to end this discussion has often been argued, but I think it causes more of a philosophical than a psychological trauma. Theory is interrupted by fact. The first words that Henry hears after the explosion are from Passini: "Oh mama mia, mama Mia. . . . Dio te salve, Maria. Dio te salve, Maria. Oh Jesus shoot me Christ shoot me mama mia mama Mia"

(55). It is possible to be both Catholic and socialist, but we are intended here to see one dogma alternate with another. Dogma and reversion—neither has the slightest effect on reality. Hemingway was a few years later to return to the subject and emphatically to rephrase its language, Passini's prayer to the Madonna being recycled in a scathing essay about the tenuousness of political beliefs in Mussolini's Italy.[24]

H. G. Wells—necessarily, I think—himself became the subject of Hemingway's questions. He appears in the long discussion (chapter 35) between Frederic Henry and Count Greffi. This dialogue is a disguise for literary criticism and also a way of allowing Hemingway to construct a certain argument. Ostensibly about Wells and the literature of 1916 and 1917, this dialogue leads us through its format of questioning to a set of implications:

> "What is there written in war-time?"
>
> "There is 'Le Feu' by a Frenchman, Barbusse. There is 'Mr. Britling Sees Through It.'"
>
> "No, he doesn't."
>
> "What?"
>
> "He doesn't see through it. Those books were at the hospital."
>
> "Then you have been reading?"
>
> "Yes, but nothing any good."
>
> "I thought 'Mr. Britling' a very good study of the English middle-class soul."
>
> "I don't know about the soul." (261)

The stated questions are important enough, but the implied questions are even more so: (1) Has any fiction yet explained the war's causes, experience, and effect? (2) Have the ideas of H. G. Wells in particular survived their moment? (3) Do those ideas—in many respects the governing ideas of the intelligentsia—actually have any explanatory power? (4) Does the empiricism of Frederic Henry have more to say than the system-making of secular religions? (5) Is his skepticism a kind of moral contaminant or, as I think it is, an intellectual virtue? These questions are, I think, the context for the last part of our own great war novel.

Mr. Britling Sees It Through was printed in many editions, earned large royalties, and early on convinced the critics that Wells's ideas were, after all, the right ideas. Most important for Hemingway's invocation of Wells, it masqueraded as the great novel of the Great War: "*The Times* announced that, 'For the first time we have a novel which touches the life of the last two years. . . . This is a really remarkable event . . . [with] nothing whatever to compare.'" According to the *Chicago Tribune,* also in 1917, it was "the best book so far published concerning the war."[25] In dismissing it, Hemingway shows more than retroactive rivalry. His own particular anxiety is to reject that influence.

Frederic Henry states that Mr. Britling sees "through" nothing. That is because Wells had superficial answers for the war, for its effects on the mind, and for human probabilities in general. He thought that character was malleable, that evil had specific social causes, and that evil was preventable if we had the right public policy. We could be educated into or out of anything. Most of all, if we are to judge from the specific language of the Hemingway dialogue, we can see through the way that history works and adjust its movement. Count Greffi's unconscious pun, picked up by Henry, becomes an argument that none of this is true.

Wells's text reminds the reader of those patriotic billposters that have been on Frederic Henry's mind. *Mr. Britling Sees It Through* is not only fiction but moral-political exhortation. The war's damage, never to be repaired and scarcely to be prevented, is viewed in a culminating passage by Wells in terms of Socialist uplift: "Let us set ourselves with all our minds and all our hearts to the perfecting and working out of the methods of democracy and the ending forever of the kings and emperors and priestcrafts . . . the traders and owners . . . who have betrayed mankind."[26] But Hemingway mistrusted that kind of theory, and he later directed readers to "read . . . *War and Peace* by Tolstoi and see how you will have to skip the big Political Thought passages, that he undoubtedly thought were the best things in the book when he wrote it, because they are no longer true or important, if they ever were more than topical." Politics in the novel, he adds, is a sure sign that a writer has given up on his talent and is hiding behind ideas.[27] Furthermore, he wants us to remember that the commentary of history is always far less honest than fiction.

Wells's kind of explanation abstracts experience; it needs Bertrand

Russell's "logical atomism" or specific explanation of causes and effects to undo its harm. And it betrays, of course, the "superstitious" quality that Russell thought characteristic of politicized discourse. In Wells, we have all the usual class suspects, but Hemingway's tragic view of life does not assign tactical guilt for the way things are. The burden of *A Farewell to Arms* is in fact that the new "social and political institutions" praised by Wells are hallucinations. Wells has a great many one-word answers for questions about the inequitable nature of life, but blaming "competition" or "aggression" (favorite culprits of his) for the unsatisfactory and even tragic nature of things does not begin to answer them.[28] For Hemingway, there is no reason in history.

The dialogue with Count Greffi is precisely *not* about progress. It rejects conventional political reasoning, refusing to assign certain norms of causation. We have already been reminded of what Mr. Britling thinks about the causes and cures of war; we are then invited to hear from a more authentic source:

> "What do you think of the war really?" I asked.
> "I think it is stupid."
> "Who will win it?"
> "Italy."
> "Why?"
> "They are a younger nation."
> "Do younger nations always win wars?"
> "They are apt to for a time."
> "Then what happens?"
> "They become older nations." (262)

First, what is not mentioned: Wellsian secular ideology named the Hun, the ruling classes, capitalism, greed, and insufficient education as prime causes of the war. War was aberrant, and what Wells called "the programme of Socialism" was a plan for offsetting such causes by changing human institutions, even human nature, in order to change history. Frederic Henry dismisses that kind of discourse because it has little descriptive and no explanatory power. In Hemingway's novel, arguments are settled existentially, by shells and bullets and monumentally irrational decisions. His characters do not adjourn into the application of theory to event. They evade, avoid, become irrational and silent, and leave discourse to the morally and politically convinced. It is not admirable but real: war does that. We want especially to recall that this is a postwar book that shares an overwhelming argument against the praise of political morality.[29] In any case, the attempt to please the "politically enlightened" is, Hemingway wrote, bound to fail since they invariably change theories, come to believe in "something else."[30]

The Count Greffi dialogue rejects conventional causes and effects, and these are visibly absent. What it does mention is equally disturbing: the causes of this war are those of other wars that have come and are to come. They are cyclical, organic to history. Although anathema to Wells (as the idea might have been to Woodrow Wilson or possibly to conventional political reasoning itself), this view carries a certain historical weight. I do not mean to imply that it is particularly dialectical, although a certain amount of theory about Western decline has been absorbed; but from the viewpoint of 1939–45, it is prescient.

It had become prescient, actually, by 1929. By then, Hemingway knew that Wells's utopian future had become the dystopian past. Hemingway's historical attitude and that of his novel were formed by events after 1917: "the rise of fascism in Italy, the effects of runaway inflation in Germany, Mustapha Kemal and the evacuation of Constantinople and Thrace, Franco-German tension in the Ruhr."[31] Hemingway was enormously well-informed about political movements, especially in Italy and Germany. These were prime examples of "younger" nations, i.e., nations consciously making the analogy between youth and political energy. "Young" is by no means an innocent phrase in the twenties and thirties, if we recall the sinister connotations of *Giovanezza* and *Jugend*. By 1929, this kind of terminology connotes healthy barbarism that renders nugatory ordinary moral judgment. Early on in 1922, Hemingway had already written that the *fascisti* who can be seen everywhere singing the hymn "Giovanezza" are "young, tough, ardent, intensely patriotic, generally good looking with the youthful beauty of the southern races, and firmly convinced that they are in the right. They have an abundance of the valor and intolerance of youth."[32] When we hear Count Greffi, we hear what is essentially the history of the future.

There are many questions in *A Farewell to Arms,* but few imply determinant answers. Both questions and answers undermine certainty. The questions that I have identified are hostile not only to religion but also to the secular systems replacing it—sometimes sequentially. Clearly, the incipient fascism of Italy comes in for a thorough examination. It is completely brutal and mindless. Other kinds of systems are not exempt: Although Hemingway may well have been on the left in the thirties, I think that he resisted its determinism in the twenties.[33] *A Farewell to Arms* takes the view that the imposition of dogma upon experience invariably falsifies.

The passage I have cited, the dialogue with Count Greffi, has the disclaimer, "I don't know about the soul." What can't be known can't be discussed—it is a restatement of the ending of Wittgenstein's *Tractatus,* which seems as useful for politics and literature as for metaphysics.

No one dances the Charleston in *The Great Gatsby,* but when the meaning of the twenties is shown on video, that is what the viewer gets. Our newspapers and magazines contain a surprising amount of reference to the twenties; it may be handy to invoke as a hallowed predecessor of ourselves. Novels, however, tend to resist generalities accounting for the way we are. Moreover, we need to resist the notion that life in the twenties was simply a kind of escape from Victorianism into materialism.

It was a complex decade whose fiction was faithful to its experience. Fitzgerald and Hemingway worked within an intellectual marketplace rich in the kind of conflict that has always been a central concern for writers. Their short fiction explores ideas taken up more fully in the novels, and I have tried to examine especially their language of inquiry. In the case of Hemingway, I have been especially concerned by the failure of explanation. His novels have a great many questions to ask, and it might reasonably be said that they are stated in the interrogative mode.

The characters of Fitzgerald and Hemingway will frequently—incessantly—ask each other questions that we know we have seen before, although not necessarily in literature. They might be called shadow questions: as stated they seem only to refer to issues in the dialogue, but they refer to large ideas beyond the dialogue. We are expected to understand the body of inference behind each statement, to read lines not as if each conveyed a finite amount of information, rather to read them for their implied connections. Questions that seem to be material and discrete—why does Jake betray himself and lose Montoya's trust? does Frederic Henry have a persuasive view of either the war or of human fate? are Tom and Daisy Buchanan simply heroically selfish?—resonate beyond the moment.

They refer themselves, I think, to the inadequacy of explanations in the life of moderns. Such questions about lives and meanings are to be read as part of the wave of philosophical inquiry about meanings that washed over the decade. The questions involve a good deal more than ethics (which are definitively unambiguous about things that demand ambiguity and because of that are unhelpful). The questions I have had in mind are about the meanings—if there are any—inhering in acts and ideas.

The twenties were disintegrative, and the search for adequate explanation was one of its great concerns, expressed over and over again by Dewey, Lippmann, Russell, Santayana, Whitehead, and Wittgenstein. All went over issues outlined by William James, and all provided for the intellectuals of the period a very difficult map to follow. The fiction of Hemingway especially is informed by such contemporary ideas. His novels are not tragic because unpleasant things happen but because (as in Whitehead's 1925 formulation) pain and suffering in a world of supposed order need to be understood, explained, and accepted. That proving impossible, Hemingway's work constitutes a view of life inexplicably endured, tragedy without tragic meaning.

NOTES

Introduction

1. C. Luther Fry and Mary Frost Jessup, "Changes in Religious Organizations," in *Recent Social Trends in the United States,* The Report of the President's Research Committee on Social Trends, 2 vols. (New York: McGraw-Hill, 1933), 2:1019.

2. Ross Posnock, "The Influence of William James on American Culture," in *The Cambridge Companion to William James,* ed. Ruth Anna Putnam (Cambridge: Cambridge University Press, 1997), 322–25.

3. Josiah Royce, "William James and the Philosophy of Life," in *The Basic Writings of Josiah Royce,* 2 vols., ed. John J. McDermott (Chicago: University of Chicago Press, 1969), 1:207. A close student of American character and history, and not one to praise overmuch, Santayana observed of Josiah Royce that "on current affairs his judgments were highly seasoned and laboriously wise." See *Santayana on America,* ed. Richard Colton Lyon (New York: Harcourt, Brace & World, 1968), 99. If that conclusion can—and should—be applied to Public Philosophy as a whole, so can some qualifications. John Dewey could be and was misinterpreted: Progressives often thought that "a new and better world" might easily be constructed around his philosophy of the "malleability" of youth. They misused Dewey in the quest to "free" man from his past—an idea that Hemingway distrusted. See Paula Fass, *The Damned and the Beautiful: American Youth in the 1920's* (New York: Oxford University Press, 1977), 30–33.

4. H. L. Mencken, *Minority Report: H. L. Mencken's Notebooks* (1956; reprint, Baltimore: Johns Hopkins University Press, 1997), 64.

5. *The Short Stories of F. Scott Fitzgerald,* ed. Matthew J. Bruccoli (New York: Charles Scribner's Sons, 1989), 51.

6. See William James, "The Will," in *The Principles of Psychology,* 2 vols., ed. Frederick H. Burkhardt (Cambridge, Mass.: Harvard University Press, 1981), 2:1167–70.

7. Ruth Anna Putnam, "Some of Life's Ideals," in *The Cambridge Companion to William James,* 289.

8. *The Short Stories of F. Scott Fitzgerald,* 33.

9. *The Impossible H. L. Mencken: A Selection of His Best Newspaper Stories,* ed. Marion Elizabeth Rodgers (New York: Anchor Books, 1991), 169–70.

10. See Fitzgerald's 1926 piece in *The Bookman* and his Introduction to the 1934 Modern Library edition of *The Great Gatsby* on Mencken's loss of influence. Both are reprinted in *F. Scott Fitzgerald on Authorship,* ed. Matthew J. Bruccoli and Judith S. Baughman (Columbia: University of South Carolina Press, 1996), 106, 139.

11. George Santayana, "Materialism and Idealism in American Life," in *Character and Opinion in the United States* (1920; reprint, New York: Doubleday Anchor, 1956), 108–9.

12. See the shrewd assessment of Belloc in Mencken, *Minority Report,* 55.

13. Reinhold Niebuhr, *Does Civilization Need Religion?* (New York: Macmillan, 1929), 205–6.

14. William James, "The Moral Philosopher and the Moral Life," in *The Will to Believe and Other Essays in Popular Philosophy,* ed. Frederick H. Burkhardt (Cambridge, Mass.: Harvard University Press, 1979), 148.

15. To Maxwell Perkins, n.d. [probably September 1928], in Edmund Wilson, *Letters on Literature and Politics, 1912–1972,* ed. Elena Wilson (New York: Farrar, Straus and Giroux, 1977), 149–51.

16. Ibid.

17. Bertrand Russell, *My Philosophical Development* (New York: Simon & Schuster, 1959), 13–14.

18. Bertrand Russell, *An Outline of Philosophy* (1927; reprint, London: Routledge, 1995), 178.

1. Cultural Drift: A Context for Fiction

1. William James, "Is Life Worth Living?" in *The Will to Believe,* 34. This famous piece, an address to the Harvard Young Men's Christian Association, was published in 1895.

2. All citations from *The Great Gatsby* refer to the edition edited by Matthew J. Bruccoli (1925; reprint, Cambridge: Cambridge University Press, 1991).

3. Jacques Barzun, *A Stroll With William James* (New York: Harper & Row, 1983), 143.

4. Ibid., 56.

5. H. L. Mencken, "Professor Veblen," in *A Mencken Chrestomathy* (New York: Alfred A. Knopf, 1967), 266, originally published in *Prejudices: First Series,* 1919.

6. See the essay "Science" by Robert H. Lowie in *Civilization in the United States,* ed. Harold E. Stearns (London: Jonathan Cape, 1922), 152–53.

7. Henry Steele Commager, cited by Alan Ryan in *John Dewey and the High Tide of American Liberalism* (New York: W. W. Norton, 1997), 19, from Henry Steele Com-

mager, *The American Mind: An Interpretation of American Thought and Character Since the 1880s* (New Haven: Yale University Press, 1950), 100.

8. For full discussion of this subject see Ronald Berman, *"The Great Gatsby" and Fitzgerald's World of Ideas* (Tuscaloosa: University of Alabama Press, 1997), passim.

9. James, "The Will," 2:1167–70.

10. William James, "Are We Automata?" *Essays in Psychology,* ed. Frederick H. Burkhardt (Cambridge, Mass.: Harvard University Press, 1983), 51.

11. Walter Lippmann, *Drift and Mastery: An Attempt To Diagnose The Current Unrest* (New York: Mitchell Kennerley, 1914), 74, 114.

12. Ibid., 331–33.

13. Ibid., xvii–xviii.

14. Ibid., 189, 197.

15. Van Wyck Brooks, *America's Coming-of-Age* (1934; reprint, Garden City, N.Y.: Doubleday Anchor, 1958), 139–44 (this volume combined three previously published essays: *America's Coming-of-Age* [1915], *Letters and Leadership* [1918], and *The Literary Life in America* [1927]). For an assessment of Brooks and the early Wilson see Sherman Paul, *Edmund Wilson* (Urbana: University of Illinois Press, 1965), 29ff.

16. Ibid., 150, 151.

17. Frederick James Smith, "Fitzgerald, Flappers and Fame," in *The Romantic Egoists,* ed. Matthew J. Bruccoli, Scottie Fitzgerald Smith, and Joan P. Kerr (New York: Charles Scribner's Sons, 1974), 79.

18. Brooks, *America's Coming-of-Age,* 120–21.

19. Royce, "William James and the Philosophy of Life," 1:215. The essay was delivered as the Phi Beta Kappa Oration at Harvard in 1911.

20. John Dewey, "Search for the Great Community," in *The Later Works, 1925–1953,* ed. Jo Ann Boydston, vol. 2 (1925–1927) (Carbondale: Southern Illinois University Press, 1984), 341.

21. Edith Wharton, *The Age of Innocence* (1920; reprint, New York: Collier Macmillan, 1987), 345–46.

22. From *Theodore Roosevelt: An American Mind,* ed. Mario R. DiNunzio (New York: Penguin Books, 1994), xiii.

23. See also John Sutherland, *The Life of Sir Walter Scott* (Oxford: Blackwell, 1995), 229ff. Sutherland states that Scott's medieval and Jacobite novels allude to current political issues in England and Scotland.

24. Brooks, *America's Coming-of-Age,* 140.

25. Ibid., 139, 140, 147. Brooks states that the phrase "feelings and desires" comes from a great Victorian, William Morris.

26. Walter Lippmann, *Public Persons* (New York: Liveright, 1976), 92.

27. Brooks, *America's Coming-of-Age,* 121–22.

28. Sinclair Lewis, *Main Street* (1920; reprint, New York: Signet, 1980), 11.

29. Lippmann, *Public Persons,* 124.

30. See Ryan, *John Dewey and the High Tide,* 149–53.

31. Sinclair Lewis, *Main Street,* 137.

32. In 1920 Fitzgerald emphasized the importance of Shaw for that "younger generation": "Just occasionally a man like Shaw who was called an immoralist 50 times worse than me back in the 90ties, lives on long enough so that the world grows up to him. What he believed in 1890 was heresy then—by now its almost respectable. . . . men of thought . . . have done more . . . than all the millions of Roosevelts and Rockerfellars." From a letter to Robert D. Clark in *F. Scott Fitzgerald: A Life in Letters,* ed. Matthew J. Bruccoli (New York: Simon & Schuster, 1995), 45.

33. All citations from "The Ice Palace" are to *The Short Stories of F. Scott Fitzgerald,* ed. Matthew J. Bruccoli (New York: Charles Scribner's Sons, 1989), 48–69.

34. Sinclair Lewis, *Main Street,* 155–57, 224

35. H. L. Mencken, *A Mencken Chrestomathy* (New York: Vintage, 1982), 188.

36. See note 19, chapter 3.

37. H. L. Mencken, "Negro Spokesman Arises to Voice His Race's Wrongs," in *The Impossible H. L. Mencken: A Selection of His Best Newspaper Stories,* ed. Marion Elizabeth Rodgers (New York: Anchor Books, 1991), 189. John J. Fishburn is identified in "The Ice Palace" (58) as one of the greatest financiers in the North, or anywhere else in the country. He may be an alter ego of James J. Hill, who had this motto: "No man on whom the snow does not fall ever amounts to a tinker's dam." Cited by Robert S. Lynd and Helen Merrell Lynd in *Middletown* (1929; reprint, San Diego: Harcourt Brace, 1957), 7. The original passage is in J. Russell Smith, *North America* (New York: Harcourt Brace, 1925), 8.

38. John Kuehl, *F. Scott Fitzgerald: A Study of the Short Fiction* (Boston: Twayne, 1991), 36.

39. See Tahita N. Fulkerson, "Ibsen in 'The Ice Palace,'" in *Fitzgerald/Hemingway Annual* 1979 (Detroit: Gale Research, 1980), 169–71.

2. "Bernice Bobs Her Hair" and the Rules

1. Santayana, "Materialism and Idealism in American Life," 104, 105–06.

2. H. L. Mencken, "The Pushful American," in *A Second Mencken Chrestomathy,* ed. Terry Teachout (New York: Alfred A. Knopf, 1995), 15. This essay was originally published as the preface to *The American Credo* by Mencken and George Jean Nathan in 1920.

3. See Robert S. Lynd and Helen Merrell Lynd, *Middletown* (1929; reprint, San Diego: Harcourt Brace, 1957), 7: in the provinces we have all the privacy of "Irvin Cobb's goldfish" bowl.

4. All citations from "Bernice Bobs Her Hair" are to *The Short Stories of F. Scott Fitzgerald,* ed. Matthew J. Bruccoli (New York: Charles Scribner's Sons, 1989), 25–47. Louis Raymond Reid, "The Small Town," in *Civilization in the United States,* ed. Harold

E. Stearns (London: Jonathan Cape, 1922), 286; Morton White, *Pragmatism and the American Mind* (New York: Oxford University Press, 1973), 22.

5. F. Scott Fitzgerald, "Winter Dreams," in *The Short Stories of F. Scott Fitzgerald*, ed. Matthew J. Bruccoli (New York: Charles Scribner's Sons, 1989), 217.

6. F. Scott Fitzgerald, "First Blood," in *The Short Stories of F. Scott Fitzgerald*, 534.

7. See Susan F. Beegel, "'Bernice Bobs Her Hair': Fitzgerald's Jazz Elegy for *Little Women*," in *New Essays on F. Scott Fitzgerald's Neglected Stories*, ed. Jackson R. Bryer (Columbia: University of Missouri Press, 1996), 58–73.

8. The passages cited are from H. L. Mencken, "Appendix on a Tender Theme" and "Venus at the Domestic Hearth," in *A Second Mencken Chrestomathy*, ed. Terry Teachout (New York: Alfred A. Knopf, 1995), 135–37.

9. H. L. Mencken, "The Feminine Mind," in *A Mencken Chrestomathy* (New York: Alfred A. Knopf, 1967), 22, originally published in *In Defense of Women*, 1918; H. L. Mencken, "The War between Man and Woman," in *A Mencken Chrestomathy*, 41, also originally published in *In Defense of Women*, 1918; H. L. Mencken, "The Woman of Tomorrow," in *The Impossible H. L. Mencken*, 181; H. L. Mencken, "A Loss to Romance," in *A Mencken Chrestomathy*, 57, originally published in *Prejudices: First Series*, 1919.

10. H. L. Mencken, *A Mencken Chrestomathy*, 64, originally published in *Prejudices: Fourth Series*, 1924.

11. F. Scott Fitzgerald, *This Side of Paradise* (1920; reprint, New York: Collier, 1986), 51.

12. Royce, "William James and the Philosophy of Life," 1:210.

13. Sigmund Freud, *The Interpretation of Dreams*, ed. James Strachey (New York: Avon, 1965), 44.

14. Ibid., xi. There were five German printings between 1900 and 1919 and two English translations.

15. "'Bernice Bobs Her Hair': Fitzgerald's Jazz Elegy for *Little Women*," in *New Essays on F. Scott Fitzgerald's Neglected Stories*, 68, 69–71.

16. All citations from *The Great Gatsby* are to the edition edited by Matthew J. Bruccoli (1925; reprint, Cambridge: Cambridge University Press, 1991).

17. This citation from the New York *Day Book* of September 7, 1852, is cited by Sacvan Bercovitch in "How to Read Melville's *Pierre*," in *Herman Melville: A Collection of Critical Essays*, ed. Myra Jehlen (Englewood Cliffs: Prentice Hall, 1994), 117.

18. D. H. Lawrence, "Fenimore Cooper's Leatherstocking Novels," in *Studies in Classic American Literature* (New York: Albert and Charles Boni, 1930), 92.

3. "The Diamond" and the Declining West

1. Wilson, *Letters on Literature and Politics*, 54.

2. H. L. Mencken, "American Culture," in *A Mencken Chrestomathy* (New York: Alfred A. Knopf, 1967), 181.

3. Edmund Wilson, "Night Thoughts in Paris: A Rhapsody," *New Republic,* March 15, 1922, 76.

4. See Sherman Paul, *Edmund Wilson* (Urbana: University of Illinois Press, 1965), 29ff.

5. See Edmund Wilson, "Gilbert Seldes and the Popular Arts," in *The Shores of Light* (New York: Farrar, Straus and Young, 1952), 164. Wilson names Brooks and H. L. Mencken as two of the great influences on his moment.

6. "Old America" is a brief section under "Letters and Leadership," in Brooks, *America's Coming-of-Age,* 91–93, originally published as *Letters and Leadership,* 1918.

7. Alexis de Tocqueville, "The Main Causes Tending to Maintain a Democratic Republic in the United States," in *Democracy in America,* ed. J. C. Mayer (New York: Anchor Books, 1969), 284. The author encounters what he believes is primeval forest, but soon detects its history: originally settled by a pioneer, "the logs he had hastily cut to build a shelter had sprouted afresh; his fences had become live hedges, and his cabin had been turned into a grove. Among the bushes were a few stones blackened by fire around a little heap of ashes; no doubt that was his hearth, covered with the ruins of a fallen chimney. For some little time I silently contemplated the resources of nature and the feebleness of man; and when I did leave the enchanted spot, I kept saying sadly: 'What! Ruins so soon!'"

8. Brooks, "Letters and Leadership," 93, 94.

9. F. Scott Fitzgerald, "Early Success," in *The Crack Up,* ed. Edmund Wilson (New York: New Directions, 1945), 87.

10. Brooks, "Letters and Leadership," 93; 94.

11. All citations from "The Diamond As Big As The Ritz" are to *The Short Stories of F. Scott Fitzgerald,* ed. Matthew J. Bruccoli (New York: Charles Scribner's Sons, 1989), 182–216.

12. Brooks, "Letters and Leadership," 111, 121.

13. Raffaello Piccoli, "As An Italian Sees It," in *Civilization in the United States,* ed. Harold E. Stearns (London: Jonathan Cape, 1922), 518 (emphasis added).

14. Ibid.

15. For a different opinion, see Robert Roulston and Helen H. Roulston, *The Winding Road to West Egg: The Artistic Development of F. Scott Fitzgerald* (Lewisburg: Bucknell University Press, 1995), 110.

16. H. W. Brands, *T. R.: The Last Romantic* (New York: Basic Books, 1997), 457.

17. Brooks, "Letters and Leadership," 92.

18. H. L. Mencken, "A Good Man in a Bad Trade," in *A Mencken Chrestomathy,* 228.

19. H. L. Mencken, "A Chance for Millionaires," in *A Mencken Chrestomathy,* 380, originally published in the New York *Evening Mail,* 1918.

20. See H. L. Mencken, *My Life as Author and Editor* (New York: Vintage, 1995), 259: "Fitz was himself no mean critic, and he saw clearly the hollowness of such notables of the time as Floyd Dell and Ernest Poole. Now and then he wrote book reviews, and

when my *Prejudices: Second Series* appeared at the end of 1920 he reviewed it for the *Bookman*."

21. *A Mencken Chrestomathy,* 178–83.

22. Roulston and Roulston, *The Winding Road to West Egg,* 111.

23. Sinclair Lewis, *Babbitt* (1922; reprint, New York: Signet, 180), 72. See also p. 58: "He had enormous and poetic admiration, though very little understanding, of all mechanical devices. They were his symbols of truth and beauty."

24. Edmund Wilson, "Current Fashions," in *The American Earthquake: A Documentary of the Twenties and Thirties* (New York: Farrar Straus Giroux, 1958), 76.

25. Walter Lippmann, *Public Opinion* (1922; reprint, New York: Free Press, 1997), 71.

26. Ibid., 72.

27. See *The Short Stories of F. Scott Fitzgerald,* 97–8.

28. Walter Lippmann, *A Preface to Morals* (New York: Macmillan, 1929), 244–45; ibid., 247.

4. *The Great Gatsby* and the Good American Life

1. *F. Scott Fitzgerald: A Life in Letters,* ed. Matthew J. Bruccoli (New York: Touchstone, 1995), 122.

2. H. L. Mencken, "Totentanz," in *A Second Mencken Chrestomathy,* ed. Terry Teachout (New York: Alfred A. Knopf, 1995), 181; Mencken, "Metropolis," 189.

3. Susan Sontag, *On Photography* (New York: Dell, 1973), 78.

4. All citations from *The Great Gatsby* in this chapter are to the edition edited by Matthew J. Bruccoli (Cambridge: Cambridge University Press, 1991).

5. Robert Emmet Long, *The Achieving of "The Great Gatsby"* (Lewisburg: Bucknell University Press, 1979), 118.

6. Lippmann, *Drift and Mastery,* xvii–xviii; from John Dewey, *The Public and its Problems* (1927), cited by Christopher Lasch in *The Revolt of the Elites* (New York: W. W. Norton, 1995), 84.

7. Royce, "William James and the Philosophy of Life," 1:215. This essay refers to the Spanish-American War of 1898.

8. Milton R. Stern, *The Golden Moment: The Novels of F. Scott Fitzgerald* (Urbana: University of Illinois Press, 1971), 247.

9. Robert Sklar, *F. Scott Fitzgerald: The Last Laocoon* (New York: Oxford University Press, 1967), 169. See also the survey of theme and idea in Richard Lehan, *"The Great Gatsby": The Limits of Wonder* (Boston: Twayne, 1990), 58–66.

10. All citations from "The Swimmers" are from *The Short Stories of F. Scott Fitzgerald,* ed. Matthew J. Bruccoli (New York: Charles Scribner's Sons, 1989).

11. Harold E. Stearns, *The Street I Know* (New York: Lee Furman, Inc., 1935), 101. See also Stearns on the enormous influence of James, Lippmann, and Santayana, 69, 98.

12. Kenneth E. Eble, *F. Scott Fitzgerald* (Boston: Twayne, 1977), 95.

13. Quoted in George Cotkin, *William James, Public Philosopher* (Baltimore: Johns Hopkins University Press, 1990), 91. See my discussion of "Success" in *"The Great Gatsby" and Modern Times* (Urbana: University of Illinois Press, 1994), 166–76.

14. Santayana, *Character and Opinion in the United States,* 108–9.

15. See my discussion of the relationship of will to act in *"The Great Gatsby" and Fitzgerald's World of Ideas,* 192–200.

16. Lippmann, *Drift and Mastery,* xvii.

17. Charles Merz, *The Great American Band Wagon* (Garden City: Garden City Publishing, 1928), 235–36.

18. See Amanda Vaill, *Everybody Was So Young: Gerald and Sara Murphy, A Lost Generation Love Story* (Boston: Houghton Mifflin, 1998), 189. There were several versions of this film.

19. See Peter Conrad, *Modern Times, Modern Places* (New York: Alfred A. Knopf, 1999), 386–87.

20. See the discussion of harmony and dissonance in early modernism by Allan Janik and Stephen Toulmin, *Wittgenstein's Vienna* (Chicago: Ivan R. Dee, 1996), 102–12. The idea of harmony as metaphor is Platonic: see section 411 of most editions of the *Republic.* I have used *The Republic,* trans. G. M. A. Grube (Indianapolis: Hackett, 1983). This section shows the correspondence between music, the individual mind, and the polity.

21. Conrad, *Modern Times, Modern Places,* 412.

22. Eliot's remarks on Stravinsky from the *Dial* (July–December 1921) and *Criterion* (October 1924) are cited in Lyndall Gordon, *T. S. Eliot: An Imperfect Life* (New York: W. W. Norton, 1998), 176.

5. "The Killers" or the Way Things Really Are

1. Kenneth S. Lynn, *Hemingway* (New York: Simon and Schuster, 1987), 112.

2. See Ernest Hemingway, "The Killers" in *The Short Stories of Ernest Hemingway: Critical Essays,* ed. Jackson J. Benson (Durham: Duke University Press, 1975), 187–91, originally published in *Understanding Poetry,* 1959.

3. B.C. Southam, *A Guide to the Selected Poems of T. S. Eliot* (San Diego: Harvest, 1994), 168–69.

4. Ruth Prigozy, "'Poor Butterfly': F. Scott Fitzgerald and Popular Music," in *Prospects: An Annual of American Cultural Studies,* ed. Jack Salzman, vol. 2 (New York: Burt Franklin, 1976), 41.

5. Mary Cass Canfield, "The Great American Art," in *Selected Vaudeville Criticism,* ed. Anthony Slide (Metuchen, N.J.: The Scarecrow Press, 1988), 225. The essay originally appeared in the *New Republic,* November 22, 1922.

6. Ibid., 226.

7. Edmund Wilson, "The Follies as an Institution," in *The American Earthquake: A Documentary of the Twenties and Thirties* (New York: Farrar Straus Giroux, 1958), 51.

8. Edmund Wilson, "Herbert Williams," in ibid., 58–59; Edmund Wilson, "Bert Savoy and Eddie Cantor of the Follies," in ibid., 59–60.

9. Gilbert Seldes, *The Seven Lively Arts* (1924; reprint, New York: Sagamore Press, 1957), 35–53. Seldes cites Eliot on Chaplin on p. 41. See Kenneth S. Lynn, *Charlie Chaplin and His Times* (New York: Simon & Schuster, 1997), 254–55, for the discussion of his appeal to "the New York intelligentsia." Lynn notes (260) that Waldo Frank's *Our America* of 1919 assigned to Chaplin a place among Dreiser, Frost, Mencken, Sherwood Anderson, and Van Wyck Brooks because he exemplified, as they did, the new movement "beyond traditional definitions of culture."

10. Seldes, *The Seven Lively Arts*, 186–87.

11. Ibid., 264.

12. Ibid., 295.

13. See Eliot's 1922 essay, "Marie Lloyd," in *Selected Prose of T. S. Eliot*, ed. Frank Kermode (New York: Harcourt Brace Jovanovich, 1975), 175: "With the decay of the music-hall, with the encroachment of the cheap and rapid-breeding cinema, the lower classes will tend to drop into the same state of protoplasm as the bourgeosie. The working man who went to the music-hall and saw Marie Lloyd. . . . will now go to the cinema . . . in that same listless apathy with which the middle and upper classes regard any entertainment of the nature of art." See Hugh Kenner, *The Invisible Poet: T. S. Eliot* (New York: Harbinger, 1959), 201–3.

14. Wilson, "Gilbert Seldes and the Popular Arts," 162–64 (emphasis added).

15. From Marshall D. Beuick, "The Vaudeville Philosopher," *The Drama* 16 (December 1925): 92–93. Reprinted in Robert W. Snyder, *The Voice of the City* (New York: Oxford University Press, 1989), 153.

16. F. Scott Fitzgerald, "Echoes of the Jazz Age," in *The Crack Up*, 18–20.

17. Snyder, *The Voice of the City*, 90.

18. Joe Laurie Jr., *Vaudeville: From the Honky-Tonks to the Palace* (New York: Henry Holt, 1953), 387.

19. Hemingway did not give Seldes credit for his ideas although he was not above using them. For the Hemingway-Seldes relationship see in chronological order Carlos Baker, *Ernest Hemingway: A Life Story* (New York: Charles Scribner's Sons, 1969), 128, 587–88, 612–13; *Ernest Hemingway: Selected Letters, 1917–1961*, ed. Carlos Baker (New York: Charles Scribner's Sons, 1981), 111, 203–4, 276, 305; Lynn, *Hemingway* (1987), 226, 235, 240, 242, 326, 351–52; Michael Reynolds, *Hemingway: The Paris Years* (Oxford: Basil Blackwell, 1989), 200, 311. Hemingway disliked Seldes because he understood him to be Jewish, a Harvard intellectual, a publishing success, and an editor who may have turned him down—in many respects, a Robert Cohn without boxing gloves. A brief passage in Lynn's biography (235) suggests that Hemingway's ideas about the lively arts probably agreed with those of Seldes.

20. Wilson, "Gilbert Seldes and the Popular Arts," 165.

21. Laurie Jr., *Vaudeville*, 81.

22. Ibid., 82.

23. All citations from "The Killers" are to *Ernest Hemingway: The Short Stories* (New York: Scribner, 1995), 279–89.

24. Bennet Musson, "A Week of One Night Stands," in *American Vaudeville as Seen by Its Contemporaries,* ed. Charles W. Stein (New York: Alfred A. Knopf, 1984), 45.

25. Laurie Jr., *Vaudeville,* 455.

26. See Scott Donaldson, "Humor in *The Sun Also Rises,*" in *New Essays on "The Sun Also Rises,"* ed. Linda Wagner-Martin (Cambridge: Cambridge University Press, 1987), 19–41.

27. Wilson, "Gilbert Seldes and the Popular Arts," 163–64.

28. Snyder, *The Voice of the City,* 138.

29. Henry F. May, *The End of American Innocence* (New York: Alfred A. Knopf, 1959), 396.

30. James, "The Moral Philosopher and the Moral Life," 148.

31. Josiah Royce, "The Philosophy of Loyalty," in *The Basic Writings of Josiah Royce,* 2 vols., ed. John J. McDermott (Chicago: University of Chicago Press, 1969), 2:864.

32. James, "The Moral Philosopher and the Moral Life," 150.

33. John Dewey, "Nature, Ends and Histories," in *The Later Works, 1925–1953,* ed. Jo Ann Boydston, vol. 1 (1925) (Carbondale: Southern Illinois University Press, 1981), 84.

34. H. L. Mencken, "The Commonwealth of Morons," in *A Second Mencken Chrestomathy* (New York: Alfred A. Knopf, 1995), 9, originally published in *Prejudices: Third Series,* 1922.

35. Ibid., 88.

36. Ibid., 245.

37. Walter Lippmann, *A Preface to Morals* (New York: Macmillan, 1929), 183–88 (emphasis added).

38. Mencken, "Professor Veblen," 266.

39. Cited by Ryan in *John Dewey and the High Tide,* 19, from Commager, *The American Mind.*

40. Ibid., 127.

41. Royce, "The Philosophy of Loyalty," 2:864–65.

42. In *William James: Writings, 1902–1910,* ed. Bruce Kuklick (New York: Library of America, 1987), 500.

43. Robert S. Lynd and Helen Merrell Lynd, *Middletown* (1929; reprint, San Diego: Harcourt Brace, 1957), 316, 330.

6. Protestant, Catholic, Jew: *The Sun Also Rises*

1. Reynolds, *Hemingway: The Paris Years,* 318.

2. Ibid., 346.

3. Michael Reynolds, *"The Sun Also Rises": A Novel of the Twenties* (Boston: Twayne Publishers, 1988), 25–6.

4. H. R. Stoneback, "In the Nominal Country of the Bogus: Hemingway's Catholi-

cism and the Biographies," in *Hemingway: Essays of Reassessment,* ed. Frank Scafella (New York: Oxford University Press, 1991), 117.

5. Hemingway owned a copy of *The Outline of History* by H. G. Wells. See Michael Reynolds, *Hemingway's Reading, 1910–1940: An Inventory* (Princeton: Princeton University Press, 1981), 199. H. G. Wells, *The Outline of History* (1920; revised, New York: MacMillan, 1921), 1096; ibid., 946; ibid., 1099.

6. *Ernest Hemingway: Selected Letters, 1917–1961,* 187, 189; ibid., 165.

7. Hilaire Belloc, *A Companion to Mr. Wells's Outline of History* (1926; revised, London: Sheed and Ward, 1929), 179.

8. Reinhold Niebuhr, *The Nature and Destiny of Man,* 2 vols. (New York: Charles Scribner's Sons, 1949) 2:164–65.

9. Belloc, *A Companion,* 228.

10. Ernest Hemingway, *The Sun Also Rises* (1926; reprint, New York: Charles Scribner's Sons, 1970), 31 (emphasis added).

11. Belloc, *A Companion,* 188.

12. See the reprint of the galleys in Frederic Joseph Svoboda, *Hemingway & "The Sun Also Rises": The Crafting of a Style* (Lawrence: University Press of Kansas, 1983), 136–37.

13. See Ernest Hemingway, *The Only Thing that Counts: The Ernest Hemingway/Maxwell Perkins Correspondence, 1925–1947,* ed. Matthew J. Bruccoli (Columbia: University of South Carolina Press, 1996). Hemingway wrote to Max Perkins on August 21, 1926, that his novel would be "altogether pointless with Belloc's name out" (44). And, on November 16, that the book "was a complete unit with all that first stuff including the Belloc episode" (48). Perkins had responded on October 30 that Hemingway "did right in taking out the first chapter and part of the second" because "almost all that is in them comes out in the story" (47). See Colin Holmes, *Anti-Semitism in British Society, 1876–1939* (London: Edward Arnold, 1979), 211.

14. Will Herberg, *Protestant-Catholic-Jew* (Garden City: Doubleday, 1955), 94.

15. See the exposition of "civil religion" by Larry E. Grimes, "Hemingway's Religious Odyssey: The Oak Park Years," in *Ernest Hemingway: The Oak Park Legacy,* ed. James Nagel (Tuscaloosa: University of Alabama Press, 1996). Grimes is exceptionally clear (pp. 40–42) on the main issue: "When religion becomes morality, church and culture merge."

16. See Bruce Barton, *The Man Nobody Knows* (Indianapolis: Bobbs-Merrill, 1929), 159–92.

17. Cited in Anthony Julius, *T. S. Eliot, Anti-Semitism, and Literary Form* (Cambridge: Cambridge University Press, 1996), 93.

18. Ibid., 146–67.

19. Michael Coren, *Gilbert: The Man Who Was G. K. Chesterton* (London: Jonathan Cape, 1989), 202–3.

20. See Bryan Cheyette, *Constructions of "The Jew" in English Literature and Society* (Cambridge: Cambridge University Press, 1993), 181–82. Cohn has not rejected

his origin or changed his religion, and neither origin nor religion are issues in the text. I have used the term "assimilated" to indicate his cultural identity, not conversion. He is depicted as a secularized American with no visible attachment to Torah.

21. From George Leonard Herter's recollections of Hemingway reprinted by H. R. Stoneback, "In the Nominal Country of the Bogus," in *Hemingway: Essays of Reassessment,* 133–34; ibid., 134, from Herter's correspondence with H. R. Stoneback.

22. See Donaldson, "Humor in *The Sun Also Rises,*" 30.

23. Michael Reynolds, "The *Sun* in Its Time: Recovering the Historical Context," in *New Essays on "The Sun Also Rises,"* ed. Linda Wagner-Martin (Cambridge: Cambridge University Press, 1987), 53–54 (emphasis added).

24. Julius, *T. S. Eliot,* 146–47.

25. Cited by Cheyette, *Constructions of "The Jew,"* 186.

26. See Julius, *T. S. Eliot,* 111–43; Cheyette, *Constructions of "The Jew,"* 62–68.

27. Julius, *T. S. Eliot,* 145.

28. The citations are from John Murray Cuddihy, *The Ordeal of Civility* (New York: Basic Books, 1974), ix, 101, 142–43.

29. Julius, *T. S. Eliot,* 144–45.

30. For an outline of anti-Semitic doctrine of the twenties see Egal Feldman, *Dual Destinies: The Jewish Encounter with Protestant America* (Urbana: University of Illinois Press, 1990), 175–88.

31. Horatio Alger Jr., *Sink or Swim* (Chicago: M. A. Donohue, n.d.), 56–58. First published 1870.

32. Horatio Alger Jr., *Strong and Steady; Or, Paddle Your Own Canoe* (Boston: Loring Publishers, 1871), 106–13.

33. When Cohn tells Jake at the end of the second chapter that he is "sick of Paris" and "sick of the Quarter," he becomes enveloped in a metaphor. At the beginning of the next chapter, Jake tells the whore Georgette that he is "sick," and she replies that "Everybody's sick. I'm sick too." The word enlarges its meaning, insists on its own extrapolation.

34. Santayana, *Character and Opinion in the United States,* 109–10.

35. W. H. Hudson, *The Purple Land* (1885; reprint, London: Duckworth, 1929), 11–12.

36. Niebuhr, *Does Civilization Need Religion?* 192–94.

37. Ibid., 205–6.

38. I have relied for my discussion of this subject on Mark Girouard's *The Return to Camelot* (New Haven: Yale University Press, 1981), 260–64. See F. Scott Fitzgerald, *The Great Gatsby,* ed. Matthew J. Bruccoli (New York: Cambridge University Press, 1991), 57. Wolfshiem and Gatsby—and Fitzgerald—share a large American interest in gentlemen and gentry that was hardly blunted by democracy. See Kim Moreland, *The Medievalist Impulse in American Literature* (Charlottesville: University Press of Virginia, 1996), 183–90. Moreland observes that if Hemingway's novel has a true chivalrous hero, that hero is Romero.

39. Girouard, *The Return to Camelot,* 263.

40. Cited in Lynn, *Hemingway,* 118.

41. Cited by Billy Altman in *Laughter's Gentle Soul: The Life of Robert Benchley* (New York: W. W. Norton, 1997), 44. Altman emphasizes Benchley's Protestant moralism.

42. See Edward F. Stanton, *Hemingway and Spain* (Seattle: University of Washington Press, 1989), 91–114.

43. See Eric Sigg, *The American T. S. Eliot* (Cambridge: Cambridge University Press, 1989), 122.

44. See Marion Meade, *Dorothy Parker: What Fresh Hell Is This?* (New York: Viking Penguin, 1989), 163ff. Dorothy Parker traveled to Europe in 1926 with Hemingway and Benchley, hoping to find a new artistic and moral environment. The trip had the elements of disaster, particularly in Spain, where she found that she loathed both the culture and the *corrida.* Hemingway, in turn, became disgusted by Parker and wrote a brutal, anti-Semitic poem about her. For the poem and a related discussion, see Lynn, *Hemingway,* 352.

45. Sigg, *The American T. S. Eliot,* 122.

46. Cited by Allen Josephs, "Hemingway's Spanish Sensibility," in *The Cambridge Companion to Ernest Hemingway,* ed. Scott Donaldson (Cambridge: Cambridge University Press, 1996), 234. From "The World Weighs a Writer's Influence," *Saturday Review* 44 (July 29, 1961) 18.

7. Order and Will in *A Farewell to Arms*

1. All citations are to *A Farewell to Arms* (1929; reprint, New York: Charles Scribner's Sons, 1957).

2. See Michael Reynolds, *Hemingway's First War* (Oxford: Basil Blackwell, 1987), 5–7; see Sigmund Freud, "Reflections Upon War and Death," from *Character and Culture,* in *Collected Papers,* ed. Philip Rieff (New York: Collier, 1963), 107–33.

3. Edmund Wilson to Maxwell Perkins, n.d. [probably September 1928], in Wilson, *Letters On Literature and Politics,* 149–51.

4. James, *Principles of Psychology,* 1:xxxi–xxxiii.

5. *The Short Stories of F. Scott Fitzgerald,* 560.

6. *The Short Stories of Ernest Hemingway,* 111, 152.

7. Lynn, *Hemingway,* 260; Reynolds, *Hemingway: The Paris Years,* 189–90; James R. Mellow, *Hemingway: A Life without Consequences* (Boston: Houghton Mifflin, 1992), 122–25. Mellow takes his subtitle (*A Life without Consequences*) from lines in this story. All of these interpretations have weight, but I have relied on his.

8. James, *Principles of Psychology,* 2:1154; ibid., 1172. See the critique of Jamesian thought in H. O. Mounce, *The Two Pragmatisms* (London: Routledge, 1997), 84–87.

9. Edmond Wilson, *I Thought of Daisy* (1929; reprint, Baltimore: Penguin Books, 1963), 125.

10. See the elegant explanation by Scott Donaldson, *By Force of Will* (New York: Viking, 1977), 151–52; and see Reynolds, *Hemingway's First War,* 82–3.

11. William James, "A World of Pure Experience," in *William James: Writings, 1902–1910,* 1159, 1160, 1182.

12. James, *Principles of Psychology,* 2:1167–68.

13. The solitary condition was once intensely valued, but note Dewey's scepticism: "no mind was ever emancipated merely by being left alone." From Dewey, "Search for the Great Community," 2:340.

14. James, *The Will to Believe,* 146.

15. John Dewey, *Classical American Philosophy,* ed. John J. Stuhr (New York: Oxford University Press, 1987), 331.

16. Dewey, "Search for the Great Community," 2:341; Wilson, *Letters on Literature and Politics,* 193; Sigmund Freud, *Civilization and Its Discontents,* ed. James Strachey (New York: W. W. Norton, 1961), 24.

17. Edmund Wilson, *Axel's Castle* (1931; reprint, New York: Charles Scribner's Sons, 1954), 5–6.

18. From "Impressionism," in *The Oxford Companion to Art,* ed. Harold Osborne (Oxford: Clarendon Press, 1970), 563.

19. From the sixth book of *The Iliad,* ed. Richmond Lattimore (Chicago: University of Chicago Press, 1951), 157.

20. This passage from *Science and the Modern World* is from *Alfred North Whitehead: An Anthology,* ed. F. S. C. Northrop and Mason W. Gross (New York: Macmillan, 1953), 445.

21. Lynn, *Hemingway,* 386.

22. Robert Evans, "Hemingway and the Pale Cast of Thought," in *Ernest Hemingway,* ed. Arthur Waldhorn (New York: McGraw-Hill, 1973), 113.

23. James, *Principles of Psychology,* 2:1167–70; William James, "Are We Automata?" in *Essays in Psychology,* 51.

24. Dewey, *The Later Works,* 2:341–42.

25. William James, "Reflex Action and Theism," in *The Will to Believe,* 110.

26. This citation from Wittgenstein's correspondence is in Marjorie Perloff, *Wittgenstein's Ladder* (Chicago: University of Chicago Press, 1996), 31. See the extensive treatment of this letter to Paul Engelmann in Ray Monk's *Ludwig Wittgenstein: The Duty of Genius* (New York: Penguin, 1991), 152–53: "If you tell me now I have no faith, you are *perfectly right,* only I did not have it before either. . . . in fact I shall either remain a swine or else I shall improve, and that's that! Only let's cut out the transcendental twaddle."

27. Cited by Samuel Hynes in *A War Imagined* (New York: Atheneum, 1991), 265.

28. *The Basic Writings of Bertrand Russell, 1903–1959,* ed. Robert E. Egner and Lester E. Denonn (New York: Simon and Schuster, 1961), 51–2.

29. See Freud, "Reflections Upon War and Death," 109; ibid, 108. According to Edith Wharton, one consequence of the war was that presumably "unalterable rules of

conduct" came to be seen "as quaintly arbitrary as the domestic rites of the Pharaohs." She cites Walter Lippmann's theory "of the country's present moral impoverishment," i.e., its severance from the imperatives of the past. In "A Backward Glance," in *Novellas and Other Writings* (1934; reprint, New York: Library of America, 1990), 780–81.

30. Cited by Carlos Baker in *Hemingway: The Writer as Artist* (Princeton: Princeton University Press, 1972), 198. Baker also describes Hemingway's reaction to postwar dictatorship in Italy and elsewhere. Regarding a Wellsian future, see Fass, *The Damned and the Beautiful,* 33. Eric Hobsbawm, *The Age of Extremes* (New York: Vintage, 1996), 109–15.

31. Isaiah Berlin, *Against the Current* (New York: Viking, 1980), 66–67.

8. Hemingway and Experience

1. See the discussion of Hemingway and journalism in Ronald Weber, *Hemingway's Art of Non-Fiction* (New York: St. Martin's Press, 1990), 6–29.

2. Baker, *Hemingway: The Writer as Artist,* 166–69. For a recent account of the imposition of "contrapuntal descriptions," see Theodore L. Gaillard Jr., "Hemingway's Debt to Cézanne: New Perspectives," *Twentieth Century Literature* 45 (Spring 1999), 65–78.

3. Ernest Hemingway, "Monologue to the Maestro: A High Seas Letter," in *By-Line: Ernest Hemingway* (New York: Touchstone, 1998), 216.

4. All citations are to *The Short Stories of Ernest Hemingway* (New York: Scribner, 1995).

5. See the first-rate discussion of Eliot's philosophy of experience in Gordon, *T. S. Eliot: An Imperfect Life,* 71–6; ibid., 75. Gordon uses the same language as Dewey about experience being innately "precarious" and our interpretation of it being artificial. Ludwig Wittgenstein, *Tractatus Logico-Philosophicus* (1922; reprint, Mineola, N.Y.: Dover, 1999), 107, from section 6.52. See Ray Monk, *Ludwig Wittgenstein: The Duty of Genius* (New York: Penguin, 1990), 287.

6. See Edmund Wilson, *I Thought of Daisy* (1929; reprint, Baltimore: Penguin Books, 1963), 133: "What a discrepancy—worst of all—what a gulf between the self which experiences and the self which writes. . . . As if there could ever be a common denominator, as if there could ever be a fusion or union, between those moments of tranquillity and our moments of pain!" A version of these lines serves as one of the epigraphs to Wilson's *The Twenties,* ed. Leon Edel (New York: Farrar, Straus and Giroux, 1975).

7. From Sidney Hook's introduction in Dewey, *The Later Works,* 1:x. Intertextuality is useful as an idea, but not infinitely extensible. The point of addressing Dewey is that he was a focus for debate: Hook points out that the "experience" issue was hotly pursued by Morris R. Cohen and also by Bertrand Russell. Dewey's ideas on experience were taken up in public lectures; they had to be defended by responses to his critics. They were transmitted to his students and reflected in his well-known "public" essays.

8. Ibid., 12–13; ibid; Dewey, "Search for the Great Community," 2:347.

9. Dewey, *The Later Works,* 1:43–47.

10. Cleanth Brooks, *The Hidden God* (New Haven: Yale University Press, 1978), 6–11.

11. Dewey, *The Later Works,* 1:45.

12. Ibid., 1:51.

13. However, see the discussion of the "response to temporality" in Larry E. Grimes, *The Religious Design of Hemingway's Early Fiction* (Ann Arbor: UMI Research Press, 1985), 106.

14. All citations are to Ernest Hemingway, *The Sun Also Rises* (New York: Charles Scribner's Sons, 1970).

15. Earl Rovit, "On Psychic Retrenchment in Hemingway," in *Hemingway: Essays of Reassessment,* ed. Frank Scafella (New York: Oxford University Press, 1991), 181–83.

16. Dewey, *The Later Works,* 1:60.

17. Hemingway, *The Only Thing that Counts,* 98–101.

18. Ibid., 227.

19. See the discussion of *The New Masses* piece by Anthony Burgess in *Ernest Hemingway* (New York: Thames and Hudson, 1999), 70–73. There is an error in this book (pp. 61–63), which is often accepted: that Hemingway's work suffers from "wordy philosophy" or "barroom metaphysics" or (many) other failed attempts at thought. Burgess values Hemingway only for image, detail, and description. But these are not independent entities, and they are made meaningful by what structures them. More important, Burgess does not understand Hemingway's negative capability, i.e., those inferences governing his refusal to state image, detail, or description because their absence constitutes an argument as well as a set of philosophical references.

20. See Perloff, *Wittgenstein's Ladder,* 62–63.

21. Ibid., 62. (The quotation is from Ludwig Wittgenstein, *Culture and Value,* ed. G. H. Von Wright [Chicago: University of Chicago Press, 1984].)

22. See the discussion of "debased language" before 1914 in Janik and Toulmin, *Wittgenstein's Vienna,* 265–69.

23. This passage from Whitehead's *The Aims of Education* cited and analyzed by Paul Grimley Kuntz in *Alfred North Whitehead* (Boston: Twayne, 1984), 29–30.

24. Wittgenstein, *Culture and Value,* 7e–8e.

25. Janik and Toulmin, *Wittgenstein's Vienna,* 265–66, 269. Janik and Toulmin argue that "the experience of our own times" is in fact implied by the reaction to cultural politics in Vienna before 1914.

26. Perloff, *Wittgenstein's Ladder,* 45.

27. See the discussion of "the instinct of destruction" in Freud, *Civilization and Its Discontents,* 66–69. The book appeared at roughly the same time as *A Farewell to Arms,* and it has some remarkable resonances.

28. Janik and Toulmin, *Wittgenstein's Vienna,* 260; ibid.; Wittgenstein, *Tractatus Logico-Philosophicus,* 88. See the discussion of "the *essence* of the thing" in Perloff, *Wittgenstein's Ladder,* 72.

29. See Niall Ferguson, "The Press Gang," in *The Pity of War* (New York: Basic Books, 1999), 234. See Lionel Trilling, *Speaking of Literature in Society* (New York: Harcourt, Brace, Jovanovich, 1980), 127–28.

30. Janik and Toulmin, *Wittgenstein's Vienna,* 269.

9. Hemingway's Questions

1. Kuntz, *Alfred North Whitehead,* 127.

2. *Alfred North Whitehead: An Anthology,* ed. Northrop and Gross, 497.

3. Josiah Royce, "Religious Questions," in *The Basic Writings of Josiah Royce,* 2 vols., ed. John J. McDermott (Chicago: University of Chicago Press, 1969), 1:384.

4. *Alfred North Whitehead: An Anthology,* 502.

5. Ibid., 364, 379–80.

6. Cited in Commager, *The American Mind,* 106. See the discussion of the decline of religion in America by Fry and Jessup, "Changes in Religious Organizations," 2:1019.

7. Eric Hobsbawm, *The Age of Empire* (Vintage: New York, 1989), 269.

8. Berlin, *Against the Current,* 115.

9. Ibid., 116.

10. All citations are to *The Short Stories of Ernest Hemingway* (New York: Scribner, 1995). Questions of two kinds structure this story. There are determinate questions, like those Nick asks his father: "can't you give her something to make her stop screaming?" (92). These kinds of questions have real answers, so the illusion is created that circumstances (including those of life itself) are explicable. But the indeterminate questions—"Why did he kill himself. . . . Do many men kill themselves. . . . Do many women. . . . Don't they ever?" (95)—have no specific answers. Nick's father has situational difficulties addressing these questions because of the limits of his life, his experience, and his knowledge. But the problem of answering such questions transcends these limits: the issue is not that he cannot find answers but that reason and faith between them cannot find answers.

11. Ryan, *John Dewey and the High Tide,* 127.

12. All citations are to *A Farewell to Arms* (New York: Charles Scribner's Sons, 1957).

13. Bertrand Russell, *Our Knowledge of the External World* (New York: W. W. Norton, 1929), 4. However, Russell's famous essay, "Why I am not a Christian" (1927) stated the naive belief that life's injustice could be fully solved and "universal happiness" attained. See this essay and "What I Believe" (1925) in *Why I Am Not a Christian* (New York: Touchstone, 1957).

14. William James, "Pragmatism," in *William James: Writings, 1902–1910,* 591.

15. Dewey, "Search for the Great Community," 2:341.

16. Russell, *My Philosophical Development,* 13–14. Russell has a relevant passage on the economy of prose: "I began to be puzzled about sentences when I was writing *The Principles of Mathematics,* and it was at that time particularly the function of verbs

that interested me. What struck me as important then was that the verb confers unity upon the sentence" (ibid., 148–50).

17. See Wittgenstein, *Tractatus Logico-Philosophicus,* 8.

18. Perloff, *Wittgenstein's Ladder,* 12.

19. Cited in ibid., 63; this brief passage, "one can only *describe* . . . ," is from Wittgenstein's *Philosophical Occasions, 1912–1951.*

20. These citations from Ludwig Wittgenstein's *Lecture on Ethics* are from Janik and Toulmin, *Wittgenstein's Vienna,* 194–95, 243.

21. Reynolds, *Hemingway's First War,* 250.

22. Michael Coren, *The Invisible Man: The Life and Liberties of H. G. Wells* (London: Bloomsbury Publishing, 1993), 142.

23. According to Geoffrey Perrett in *America in the Twenties* (New York: Simon & Schuster, 1982), 51, Rose Pastor Stokes, a feminist and Socialist, received a ten-year sentence in 1918 for writing in the *Kansas City Star,* "I am for the people and the government is for the profiteers." President Wilson tried to jail the editor for running her piece.

24. See the account of death and ideology in Ernest Hemingway, "Wings Always over Africa: An Ornithological Letter," in *By-Line: Ernest Hemingway,* 229–30, originally published in *Esquire,* January 1936: "The principal expression that one recalls as hearing from the lips, mouths, or throats of wounded Italians was the words, '*Mamma mia! Oh mamma mia!*' The lightly wounded are more apt to say, "Duce! I salute you Duce! I am happy to die for you, Oh Duce!" But when a soldier is badly wounded and says, "*Oh Mamma mia* . . . the Duce will be far from his thoughts."

25. Cited in Coren, *The Invisible Man,* 141.

26. Cited in David C. Smith, *H. G. Wells: Desperately Mortal* (New Haven: Yale University Press, 1986), 222.

27. Ernest Hemingway, "Old Newsman Writes: A Letter from Cuba," in *By-Line: Ernest Hemingway,* 184, originally published in *Esquire,* December 1934.

28. David C. Smith, *H. G. Wells: Desperately Mortal,* 223; ibid., 223–24.

29. Pre-war writing deserves attention as well: see Niall Ferguson's essay on literature and war, "The Mythos of Militarism," in *The Pity of War* (New York: Basic Books, 1999), 1–30.

30. Ernest Hemingway, "Old Newsman Writes: A Letter from Cuba" in *By-Line: Ernest Hemingway,* 184.

31. Kenneth Kinnamon, "Hemingway and Politics," in *The Cambridge Companion to Ernest Hemingway,* ed. Scott Donaldson (New York: Cambridge University Press, 1996), 150.

32. Ernest Hemingway, "Genoa Conference," in *By-Line: Ernest Hemingway,* 28, originally published in the *Toronto Daily Star,* April 13, 1922.

33. See Kinnamon, "Hemingway and Politics," 157–59.

SELECT BIBLIOGRAPHY

Alger Jr., Horatio. *Sink or Swim*. Chicago: M. A. Donohue, n.d.

———. *Strong and Steady; Or, Paddle Your Own Canoe*. Boston: Loring Publishers, 1871.

Baker, Carlos. *Hemingway: The Writer as Artist*. Princeton: Princeton University Press, 1972.

Beegel, Susan F. "'Bernice Bobs Her Hair': Fitzgerald's Jazz Elegy for *Little Women*." In *New Essays on F. Scott Fitzgerald's Neglected Stories*, edited by Jackson R. Bryer. Columbia: University of Missouri Press, 1996.

Belloc, Hilaire. *A Companion to Mr. Wells's Outline of History*. 1926. Revised. London: Sheed and Ward, 1929.

Benson, Jackson J., ed. *The Short Stories of Ernest Hemingway: Critical Essays*. Durham: Duke University Press, 1975.

Berlin, Isaiah. *Against the Current*. New York: Viking, 1980.

Berman, Ronald. *"The Great Gatsby" and Fitzgerald's World of Ideas*. Tuscaloosa: University of Alabama Press, 1997.

———. *"The Great Gatsby" and Modern Times*. Urbana: University of Illinois Press, 1994.

Brands, H. W. *T. R.: The Last Romantic*. New York: Basic Books, 1997.

Brooks, Van Wyck. *America's Coming-of-Age*. 1934. Reprint. Garden City: Doubleday Anchor, 1958.

Burgess, Anthony. *Ernest Hemingway*. New York: Thames and Hudson, 1999.

Cheyette, Bryan. *Constructions of "The Jew" in English Literature and Society*. Cambridge: Cambridge University Press, 1993.

Conrad, Peter. *Modern Times, Modern Places*. New York: Alfred A. Knopf, 1999.

Dewey, John. *The Later Works, 1925–1953*. Edited by Jo Ann Boydston. Vol. 1

(1925) and vol. 2 (1925–1927). Carbondale: Southern Illinois University Press, 1981, 1984.

Donaldson, Scott. *The Cambridge Companion to Ernest Hemingway.* Cambridge: Cambridge University Press, 1996.

Ferguson, Niall. *The Pity of War.* New York: Basic Books, 1999.

Fitzgerald, F. Scott. *The Crack Up.* Edited by Edmund Wilson. New York: New Directions, 1945.

———. *F. Scott Fitzgerald on Authorship.* Edited by Matthew J. Bruccoli and Judith S. Baughman. Columbia: University of South Carolina Press, 1996.

———. *The Great Gatsby.* Edited by Matthew J. Bruccoli. 1925. Reprint. Cambridge: Cambridge University Press, 1991.

———. *A Life in Letters.* Edited by Matthew J. Bruccoli. New York: Simon & Schuster, 1995.

———. *The Short Stories of F. Scott Fitzgerald.* Edited by Matthew J. Bruccoli. New York: Charles Scribner's Sons, 1989.

Freud, Sigmund. *Civilization and Its Discontents.* Edited by James Strachey. New York: W. W. Norton, 1961.

———. *The Interpretation of Dreams.* Edited by James Strachey. New York: Avon, 1965.

———. "Reflections Upon War and Death," from *Character and Culture.* In *Collected Papers.* Edited by Philip Rieff. New York: Collier, 1963.

Fry, C. Luther, and Mary Frost Jessup. "Changes in Religious Organizations." In *Recent Social Trends in the United States.* The Report of the President's Research Committee on Social Trends. 2 vols. New York: McGraw-Hill, 1933.

Girouard, Mark. *The Return to Camelot.* New Haven: Yale University Press, 1981.

Gordon, Lyndall. *T. S. Eliot: An Imperfect Life.* New York: W. W. Norton, 1998.

Hemingway, Ernest. *By-Line: Ernest Hemingway.* New York: Touchstone, 1998.

———. *Ernest Hemingway: Selected Letters, 1917–1961.* Edited by Carlos Baker. New York: Charles Scribner's Sons, 1981.

———. *Ernest Hemingway: The Short Stories.* New York: Scribner, 1995.

———. *A Farewell to Arms.* 1929. Reprint. New York: Charles Scribner's Sons, 1957.

———. *The Only Thing that Counts: The Ernest Hemingway/Maxwell Perkins Correspondence, 1925–1947.* Edited by Matthew J. Bruccoli. Columbia: University of South Carolina Press, 1996.

———. *The Sun Also Rises.* New York: Charles Scribner's Sons, 1970.

Herberg, Will. *Protestant-Catholic-Jew.* Garden City: Doubleday, 1955.

James, William. *Essays in Psychology.* Edited by Frederick H. Burkhardt. Cambridge, Mass.: 1983.

———. *The Principles of Psychology.* Edited by Frederick H. Burkhardt. 2 vols. Cambridge, Mass.: Harvard University Press, 1981.

———. *William James: Writings, 1902–1910.* Edited by Bruce Kuklick. New York: Library of America, 1987.

———. *The Will to Believe and Other Essays in Popular Philosophy.* Edited by Frederick H. Burkhardt. Cambridge, Mass.: Harvard University Press, 1979.

Janik, Allan, and Toulmin, Stephen. *Wittgenstein's Vienna.* Chicago: Ivan R. Dee, 1996.

Julius, Anthony. *T. S. Eliot, Anti-Semitism, and Literary Form.* Cambridge: Cambridge University Press, 1996.

Laurie Jr., Joe. *Vaudeville: From the Honky-Tonks to the Palace.* New York: Henry Holt, 1953.

Lehan, Richard. *"The Great Gatsby": The Limits of Wonder.* Boston: Twayne, 1990.

Lewis, Sinclair. *Babbitt.* 1922. Reprint. New York: Signet, 1980.

———. *Main Street.* 1920. Reprint. New York: Signet, 1980.

Lippmann, Walter. *Drift and Mastery: An Attempt To Diagnose The Current Unrest.* New York: Mitchell Kennerly, 1914.

———. *A Preface to Morals.* New York: Macmillan, 1929.

———. *Public Opinion.* 1922. Reprint, New York: Free Press, 1997.

———. *Public Persons.* New York: Liveright, 1976.

Long, Robert Emmet. *The Achieving of "The Great Gatsby."* Lewisburg: Bucknell University Press, 1979.

Lynd, Robert S., and Helen Merrell Lynd. *Middletown: A Study of Modern American Culture.* New York: Harcourt Brace, 1929.

Lynn, Kenneth S. *Hemingway.* New York: Simon and Schuster, 1987.

Mellow, James R. *Hemingway: A Life without Consequences.* Boston: Houghton Mifflin, 1992.

Mencken, H. L. *The Impossible H. L. Mencken: A Selection of His Best Newspaper Stories.* Edited by Marion Elizabeth Rodgers. New York: Anchor Books, 1991.

———. *A Mencken Chrestomathy.* New York: Vintage, 1982.

———. *Minority Report: H. L. Mencken's Notebooks.* 1956. Reprint. Baltimore: Johns Hopkins University Press, 1977.

———. *My Life as Author and Editor.* Edited by Jonathan Yardley. New York: Vintage, 1995.

———. *A Second Mencken Chrestomathy.* Edited by Terry Teachout. New York: Alfred A. Knopf, 1995.

Merz, Charles. *The Great American Band Wagon.* Garden City: Garden City Publishing, 1928.

Monk, Ray. *Ludwig Wittgenstein: The Duty of Genius.* New York: Penguin, 1990.

Nagel, James, ed. *Ernest Hemingway: The Oak Park Years.* Tuscaloosa: University of Alabama Press, 1996.

Niebuhr, Reinhold. *Does Civilization Need Religion?* New York: Macmillan, 1929.

———. *The Nature and Destiny of Man.* 2 vols. New York: Charles Scribner's Sons, 1949.

Perloff, Marjorie. *Wittgenstein's Ladder.* Chicago: University of Chicago Press, 1996.

President's Research Committee on Social Trends, *Recent Social Trends in the United States.* New York: McGraw-Hill, 1933.

Prigozy, Ruth. "'Poor Butterfly': F. Scott Fitzgerald and Popular Music." In *Prospects: An Annual of American Cultural Studies.* Edited by Jack Salzman. Vol. 2, 41–67. New York: Burt Franklin, 1976.

Putnam, Ruth Anna, ed. *The Cambridge Companion to William James.* Cambridge: Cambridge University Press, 1997.

Reynolds, Michael. *Hemingway: The Paris Years.* Oxford: Basil Blackwell, 1989.

———. *Hemingway's First War.* Oxford: Basil Blackwell, 1987.

———. *Hemingway's Reading, 1910–1940: An Inventory.* Princeton: Princeton University Press, 1981.

———. *"The Sun Also Rises": A Novel of the Twenties.* Boston: Twayne Publishers, 1988.

Royce, Josiah. *The Basic Writings of Josiah Royce.* Edited by John J. McDermott. 2 vols. Chicago: University of Chicago Press, 1969.

Russell, Bertrand. *The Basic Writings of Bertrand Russell, 1903–1959.* Edited by Robert E. Egner and Lester E. Denonn. New York: Simon and Schuster, 1961.

———. *An Outline of Philosophy.* 1927. Reprint. London: Routledge, 1995.

———. *My Philosophical Development.* New York: Simon & Schuster, 1959.

Ryan, Alan. *John Dewey and the High Tide of American Liberalism.* New York: W. W. Norton, 1997.

Santayana, George. *Character and Opinion in the United States.* 1920. Reprint. New York: Doubleday Anchor, 1956.

———. *Santayana on America.* Edited by Richard Colton Lyon. New York: Harcourt, Brace & World, 1968.

Scafella, Frank, ed. *Hemingway: Essays of Reassessment.* New York: Oxford University Press, 1991.

Seldes, Gilbert. *The Seven Lively Arts.* 1924. Reprint. New York: Sagamore Press, 1957.

Sigg, Eric. *The American T. S. Eliot.* Cambridge: Cambridge University Press, 1989.

Slide, Anthony, ed. *Selected Vaudeville Criticism.* Metuchen, N.J.: The Scarecrow Press, 1988.

Smith, David C. *H. G. Wells: Desperately Mortal.* New Haven: Yale University Press, 1986.

Snyder, Robert W. *The Voice of the City.* New York: Oxford University Press, 1989.

Sontag, Susan. *On Photography.* New York: Dell, 1973.

Stern, Milton R. *The Golden Moment: The Novels of F. Scott Fitzgerald* (Urbana: University of Illinois Press, 1971),

Stearns, Harold, ed. *Civilization in the United States.* New York: Harcourt Brace, 1922.

Stein, Charles W., ed. *American Vaudeville as Seen by Its Contemporaries.* New York: Alfred A. Knopf, 1984.

Svoboda, Frederic Joseph. *Hemingway & "The Sun Also Rises": The Crafting of a Style.* Lawrence: University Press of Kansas, 1983.

Wagner-Martin, Linda, ed. *New Essays on "The Sun Also Rises."* Cambridge: Cambridge University Press, 1987.

Wells, H. G. *The Outline of History.* 1920. Revised. New York: MacMillan, 1921.

Whitehead, Alfred North. *Alfred North Whitehead: An Anthology,* ed. F.S.C. Northrop and Mason W. Gross. New York: Macmillan, 1953.

Wilson, Edmund. *The American Earthquake: A Documentary of the Twenties and Thirties.* New York: Farrar Straus Giroux, 1958.

———. *Axel's Castle.* 1931. Reprint. New York: Charles Scribner's Sons, 1954.

———. *Letters on Literature and Politics, 1912–1972.* Edited by Elena Wilson. New York: Farrar, Straus and Giroux, 1977.

———. *The Shores of Light.* New York: Farrar, Straus and Young, 1952.

Wittgenstein, Ludwig. *Culture and Value.* Edited by G. H. Von Wright. Chicago: University of Chicago Press, 1984.

———. *Tractatus Logico-Philosophicus.* Mineola: Dover, 1999.

INDEX

Alger, Horatio, Jr., 92

Baker, Carlos, 116
Barzun, Jacques: on Henry James, 12
Beegel, Susan, 37
Belloc, Hilaire, 84–86, 159 (n. 13)
Benchley, Robert, 96–97
Berlin, Isaiah: moral order, 115, 134–35
Brands, H. W., 44
Brooks, Cleanth, 120
Brooks, Van Wyck: "the acquisitive life," 26, 43–44; American landscape, 41–43; commercialism, 44; drift, 15–21; materialism, 26; pioneering, 43; William James, 16
Burgess, Anthony, 164 (n. 19)

Canfield, Mary Cass, 66
Chattaway, Thurland, 65
Chesterton, G. K., 88, 90, 91
Cheyette, Bryan, 87
Chicago Tribune, 144
Civilization in the United States: plutocracy, 44; "The Small Town," 29; William James, 12–13
Commager, Henry Steele: John Dewey, 13, 79
Copeland, Aaron, 64
Coren, Michael, 88
Crowley, Alister, 85–86
cultural drift, 11–27, 109–11

Daily Mirror, 130
Dewey, John: drift, 18, 109; experience, 105, 110, 118–23; idea of meaning, 77, 79; language, 106; loyalties, 54; moral order, 76–77; politics and religion, 138
dialogue, 135–36
dissonance, 62–64
Donaldson, Scott, 89

Eliot, T. S.: anti-Semitism, 87–90; dissonance, 64; *Knowledge and Experience,* 118; "music-hall comedian," 68–69, 157 (n. 13); reality, 118; *The Waste Land,* 65, 94

Fitzgerald, F. Scott: "Bernice Bobs Her Hair," 3–4, 28–39; "The Diamond As Big As The Ritz," 40–51; "Emotional Bankruptcy," 101; "First Blood," 32; George Bernard Shaw, 152 (n. 32); *The Great Gatsby,* 5–6, 11–12, 15, 17–18, 26–27, 38, 52–64; "The Ice Palace," 3, 21–27; "The Swimmers," 56; twenties, 69
Freud, Sigmund: civilization, 129; disillusionment, 99, 114; *The Interpretation of Dreams,* 35–37; isolation, 106; repression, 114

"Giovanezza," 146
Girouard, Mark, 95–96
Gordon, Lyndall, 118

Hammerstein, Willie, 70
Hemingway, Ernest: "A Clean, Well-Lighted Place," 136; *A Farewell to Arms,* 8–9, 99–115, 123, 128–29, 136–47; "A Natural History of the Dead," 123; anti-Semitism, 89–91; "Big Two-Hearted River," 125; "The Capital of the World," 142; catholicism, 82–88, 121; "The End of Something," 102; experience, 116–31; Gilbert Seldes, 157 (n. 19); *The Green Hills of Africa,* 116; H. G. Wells, 143–47; Hilaire Belloc, 159 (n. 13); "Indian Camp," 135–36, 165 (n. 10); "The Killers," 7–8, 65–81, 135–36; questions, 132–47; "The Short Happy Life of Francis Macomber," 102; "The Snows of Kilimanjaro," 124; socialism, 141–47; "Soldier's Home," 86, 102, 117–18; *The Sun Also Rises,* 6–7, 82–98, 121–23, 125–28; "The Undefeated," 117; *War and Peace,* 144
Hemingway, Grace Hall, 96
Herberg, Will, 86
Hobsbawm, Eric, 115, 134
Hudson, W. H.: *The Purple Land,* 91–94
Huysmanns, J. K., 87

James, William: consciousness, 13; drift, 4, 13, 109; energy, 13; influence of, 2–3, 79; metaphysics, 138; moral order, 8, 75, 76; moral solitude, 104–5, 110; *Pragmatism,* 80–81; subjectivity, 105; success, 56–57; will, 3, 101, 103–5, 109
Janik, Allan (and Stephen Toulmin), 128–31
Julius, Anthony, 87–91

Kipling, Rudyard, 91

Laurie, Joe, Jr., 70, 71
Lawrence, D. H., 39
Lewis, Sinclair: *Babbitt,* 24, 47, 155 (n. 23); *Main Street,* 21–23
Lippmann, Walter: "acquisitive instinct," 51; anti-Semitism, 91; drift, 62; *Drift and Mastery,* 14–15; Jane Addams, 22; marketplace values, 48–49, 51; moral order, 54, 78; Sinclair Lewis, 20–21
Little Women, 32
Lloyd George, David, 130
Long, Robert Emmet, 54
Lord Northcliffe, 130
Lynn, Kenneth S., 65, 102, 108

Madariaga, Salvador de, 98
May, Henry F., 74
Mellow, James R., 102
Mencken, H. L.: American women, 4, 33–34; F. Scott Fitzgerald, 154–55 (n. 20); George Santayana, 3; Hilaire Belloc, 150 (n. 12); metropolis, 52–53; moral order, 77; plutocracy, 40, 45–47; the South, 24–26; William James, 12, 79
Merz, Charles, 62–63
Middletown, 80
Murphy, Gerald, 63–64

Niebuhr, Reinhold: Albert Schweitzer, 94; Herbert Spencer, 94–95; idea of progress, 85; Protestant idealism, 94–95; tragic sense of history, 7, 94

Parker, Dorothy, 98, 161 (n. 44)
Perkins, Max, 123–24
Perloff, Marjorie, 128–29, 139
Pfeiffer, Pauline, 82–83
Poliakov, Léon, 91
Prigozy, Ruth, 65

Reid, Louis Raymond, 29
Research Committee on Social Trends, 1–2
Reynolds, Michael, 82–83, 89, 99, 102, 141
Roosevelt, Theodore, 18–19
Rovit, Earl, 122
Royce, Josiah: American Dream, 17, 55; moral order, 75, 80; provinces, 29; psychology, 35–36; William James, 3
Russell, Bertrand: descriptive reality, 138; idea of progress, 113; language and fact, 9, 139, 145; religion, 165 (n. 13)

Santayana, George: American society, 4, 28; Josiah Royce, 149 (n. 3); materialism and idealism, 57–58; Protestant idealism, 93, 98
Seldes, Gilbert: *The Seven Lively Arts,* 66–69; vaudeville, 70
Sontag, Susan, 53
Stearns, Harold E., 56
Stern, Milton R., 55
Stoneback, H. R., 83

Tillich, Paul, 120
Times of London, 144
Tocqueville, Alexis de, 42, 154 (n. 7)
Tufts, James H., 134

Vaill, Amanda, 63–64
Vanity Fair, 49–50
vaudeville: performers, 67–74; philosophy, 69; scripts, 70–74
Victoria Theatre, 70
vital energy, 61–62

Webb, Beatrice, 111–12
Wells, H. G.: idea of progress, 84–85; *Mr. Britling Sees It Through,* 143–45; *The Outline of History,* 83–85; socialism, 142–47
Wharton, Edith: *Age of Innocence,* 18–20; reality, 19–20
White, Morton, 29
Whitehead, Alfred North: experience, 127, 133; moral order, 133; religion, 132; *Religion in the Making,* 132–33; *Science and the Modern World,* 133; subjectivity, 108
Wilson, Edmund: American landscape, 40–41; A. N. Whitehead, 106, 108; *Axel's Castle,* 106; books about America, 40; experience, 163 (n. 6); mechanical progress, 48; pointlessness, 73; romanticism, 106–7; subjectivity, 8, 100, 106; vaudeville, 66–69, 70; will, 9, 100–101, 103

Wister, Owen, 123
Wittgenstein, Ludwig: experience, 129–31, 140; knowledge, 147; language, 125, 128–31, 139, 141; ritual, 125; self-consciousness, 110–11; silence, 128, 139; understanding, 118

ABOUT THE AUTHOR

RONALD BERMAN is Professor of Literature, University of California at San Diego. He earned his bachelor's degree from Harvard and his doctorate from Yale. He served as Chairman of the National Endowment for the Humanities from 1971 to 1977 and was awarded the Medal of the City of New York. Among his most recent publications are *"The Great Gatsby" and Modern Times* (1996) and *"The Great Gatsby" and Fitzgerald's World of Ideas* (1997), winner of the 1995 Elizabeth Agee Prize in American Literature.